History of Malaysia

A Captivating Guide to Ancient Kingdoms, Colonial Melaka, Modernization, and the Post-Independence Years

© Copyright 2024 - All rights reserved.

The content contained within this book may not be reproduced, duplicated, or transmitted without direct written permission from the author or the publisher.

Under no circumstances will any blame or legal responsibility be held against the publisher, or author, for any damages, reparation, or monetary loss due to the information contained within this book, either directly or indirectly.

Legal Notice:

This book is copyright protected. It is only for personal use. You cannot amend, distribute, sell, use, quote, or paraphrase any part, or the content within this book, without the consent of the author or publisher.

Disclaimer Notice:

Please note the information contained within this document is for educational and entertainment purposes only. All effort has been executed to present accurate, up-to-date, reliable, and complete information. No warranties of any kind are declared or implied. Readers acknowledge that the author is not engaging in the rendering of legal, financial, medical, or professional advice. The content within this book has been derived from various sources. Please consult a licensed professional before attempting any techniques outlined in this book.

By reading this document, the reader agrees that under no circumstances is the author responsible for any losses, direct or indirect, that are incurred as a result of the use of the information contained within this document, including, but not limited to, errors, omissions, or inaccuracies.

Free Bonus from Captivating History (Available for a Limited time)

Hi History Lovers!

Now you have a chance to join our exclusive history list so you can get your first history ebook for free as well as discounts and a potential to get more history books for free!

Simply visit the link below to join.

Or, Scan the QR code!

captivatinghistory.com/ebook

Also, make sure to follow us on Facebook, X, and YouTube by searching for Captivating History.

Table of Contents

INTRODUCTION 1
CHAPTER 1 - OF MYTHS AND LEGENDS: THE ANCIENT POWERS OF THE MALAY PENINSULA 4
CHAPTER 2 - ADRUJA WIJAYAMALA SINGA: THE UNSUNG HEROINE OF HISTORY 12
CHAPTER 3 - THE ESTABLISHMENT OF MELAKA 19
CHAPTER 4 - THE LEGEND OF HANG TUAH 27
CHAPTER 5 - THREATS FROM FARAWAY LANDS......................35
CHAPTER 6 - THE START OF BRITISH INTERVENTION 45
CHAPTER 7 - THE STRUGGLES IN BORNEO.................................55
CHAPTER 8 - THE JAPANESE INVASION 66
CHAPTER 9 - THE END OF THE JAPANESE OCCUPATION 73
CHAPTER 10 - THE FEDERATION OF MALAYA AND THE COMMUNIST INSURGENCY OF THE MALAYAN NATIONAL LIBERATION ARMY 80
CHAPTER 11 - THE LIGHT AT THE END OF THE TUNNEL........87
CHAPTER 12 - POST-INDEPENDENCE AND THE ESTABLISHMENT OF MALAYSIA 93
CONCLUSION 98
HERE'S ANOTHER BOOK BY CAPTIVATING HISTORY THAT YOU MIGHT LIKE 101
FREE BONUS FROM CAPTIVATING HISTORY (AVAILABLE FOR A LIMITED TIME) 102
REFERENCE LIST 103

Introduction

Long before the existence of the iconic Petronas Twin Towers and the sky-piercing Merdeka 118, centuries before the birth of the very first sultanate in Southeast Asia, and ages before the formation of the nation itself, the Malay Peninsula and the surrounding archipelago, especially the strategic Straits of Malacca, were known not only as a melting pot of different cultures and knowledge but also as a bustling center of trade and commerce. The region's tropical rainforests provided an unimaginable amount of natural resources, while the western part of the peninsula, specifically, was renowned for its abundant resources of tin, which, along with gold and aromatic spices, were highly sought after in both the Indian and Chinese markets.

Before the name "Malaysia" was etched onto maps and books of records, the peninsula was known by many names. The Greek geographer Claudius Ptolemy referred to it as the Golden Chersonese, and the peninsula was identified as Malayadvipa in the ancient Indian text *Ramayana*. The Yuan and Ming dynasties, on the other hand, used the terms Bok-la-Yu and Wu-lai-yu. Marco Polo, the famous Venetian traveler, mentioned the name Malauir to reference a kingdom on the peninsula. Much later on, the Portuguese used the term Terra de Tana Malaio. These different terms are evidence that the region was able to polish its reputation over time, eventually putting it on the stage of international prominence and acclaim, even though the peninsula was situated far from the colossal powers of ancient times, such as the vast Roman or Chinese empires.

But, of course, every story has a beginning. In the past, these regions were a broad canvas painted with a series of stories, intrigues, and power plays. The rainforests and coastal areas also echo with a rich history, some of which are infused with myths and legends passed down from one generation to the next. The foundation of Langkasuka, one of the oldest kingdoms on the peninsula, for example, is a fascinating story that blends both facts and legends, making it one of the most intriguing tales ever recorded in the annal of Malaysian history. The tales of Merong Mahawangsa and Adruja Wijayamala Singa straddle the line between history and legend, serving as a testament to the Malay Peninsula's early allure—an allure that attracted traders, adventurers, and conquerors from far and wide.

As we venture further into the narrative, the establishment of the Melaka Sultanate marks a pivotal chapter. This is not merely a tale of the rise of a kingdom but rather the birth of a strategic maritime empire whose influence permeated throughout the region, affecting trade, politics, and culture. The legacy of Melaka set the stage for the storied strait to become a nautical crossroads coveted by European powers. It is here that the tale takes a turn, as the first European colonists, the Portuguese and then the Dutch, cast their anchors upon the peninsula's shores, bringing with them the winds of change that would forever alter the region's trajectory.

Malaysia's historical fabric becomes even more intricate with the arrival of the British, an era marked by colonial ambitions, economic transformations, and the indelible imprint of Western influence. This period, however, was not just defined by the forces of colonialism but also by the indomitable spirit of resistance within the local population. Heroes such as Dato' Maharaja Lela and Mat Kilau in the Malay Peninsula, alongside Mat Salleh and Rentap in Borneo, became icons of defiance against colonial rule.

Yet, the Malayans were still far from achieving peace. Their resilience was tested further during the harrowing years of Japanese occupation, a time when the people of Malaya were subjected to untold brutality and bloodshed. These tough times left a lasting mark on the country's memory, showing how strong its people were when facing great hardship. It was only after World War II that the road to independence became clearer in the eyes of the Malayans.

Malaysia may not have millennia of recorded history like some of the ancient civilizations of the world, yet it possesses a distinct identity that is as rich and complex as any. In its relatively brief history, Malaysia has managed to forge a unique cultural identity, one that is a testament to the confluence of the many ethnicities, languages, and religions that have come together in this vibrant land. This book strives to honor Malaysia's rich heritage rather than playing a hand in letting it fade into the sands of time. It seeks to illuminate the stories of its people and the myriad influences that have shaped its present. Through these pages, readers are invited to explore the grand narrative of a nation that, though young in years, stands tall with a spirit and legacy that rivals the oldest of histories.

Chapter 1 - Of Myths and Legends: The Ancient Powers of the Malay Peninsula

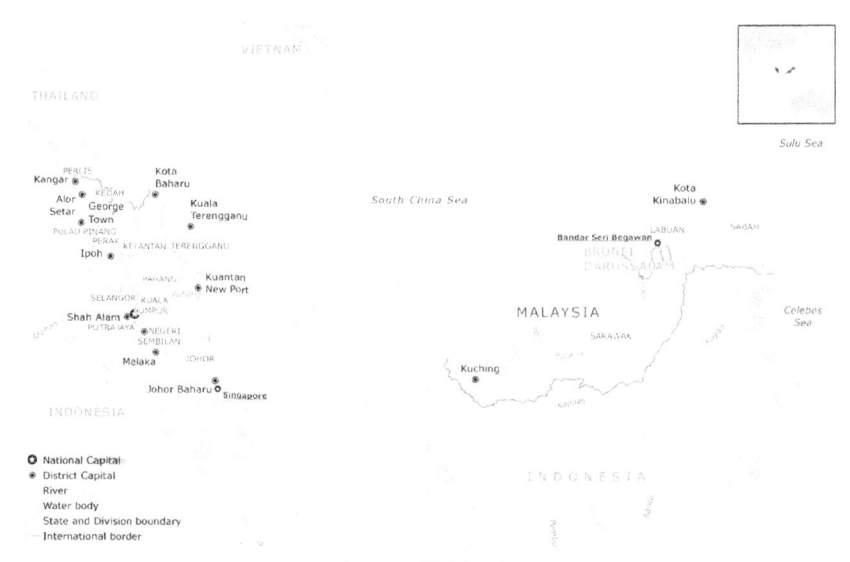

A map of Malaysia.
JRC, ECHO, EC, CC BY 4.0 <https://creativecommons.org/licenses/by/4.0>, via Wikimedia Commons: https://commons.wikimedia.org/wiki/File:Malaysia_Base_Map.png

Our story is believed to have begun in the west, far amidst the grand columns of the Eternal City, Rome. However, the exact year is unknown since the details are long gone, eaten by unruly Father Time himself.

However, we can safely assume that this event took place sometime in the early 2nd century CE, long after the Romans were introduced to their very first emperor. Indeed, the empire was almost constantly involved in multiple series of wars and conquests, but as violent as the Roman legions were, the Romans often played at forging peaceful alliances with other powerful forces.

According to Malay tales and legends, the Roman emperor (or the "King of Rome" in these sources) had heard of a colossal power far beyond the borders of Europe. Through information gathered by his men, the emperor was made aware of the empire of China. In the eyes of the Roman emperor, this empire—albeit only learning of its existence through secondhand accounts—was worth a friendly relationship. Its wealth and power could probably be of use someday. And so, the Roman emperor began seeking ways to secure an alliance with the Chinese.

Many days were spent discussing and arguing over strategies to forge the relationship between the two empires. Finally, with the support of his advisors, the emperor decided that the best way to achieve the goal was through the sacred bond of matrimony between his son and the daughter of the Chinese emperor. Many agreed to the decision; however, unbeknownst to the Romans, there was one particular creature that was far from content with the union between the two empires. This creature was an egoistic phoenix that the Malays referred to as the "Garuda."

Confident that it was absolutely impossible for two individuals from distant lands to unite under the name of marriage, the Garuda was intent on interrupting the wedding. It quickly flapped its giant wings and journeyed to the Asian continent, where it set eyes on the Chinese princess peacefully living her royal life surrounded by her most loyal servants. Without a moment of hesitation, the Garuda kidnapped the princess—some said the phoenix even got a hold of her servants—and brought her to an island on the Andaman Sea known as Langkapuri (presumably modern-day Langkawi). Here, the princess was given a treatment fit for a royal. The Garuda did not provide a palace for her to call home, but the creature also granted each of her requests, except for returning to her homeland, of course.

The wind eventually blew news of the missing princess to the west, startling the Roman emperor. With great haste, he gathered his advisors for a discussion about their next move. The Romans were not familiar with the idea of defeat, so they moved quickly to ensure their plans were back on track. Considering each suggestion voiced by his most loyal advisors, the Roman emperor announced that he decided to send his prince and a fleet full of his best Roman soldiers to search for the Chinese princess. Of course, sailing to such a distant land required a formidable leader at the helm. Therefore, the Roman ruler called upon one particular man who went by the name of Merong Mahawangsa.

An illustration of a Balinese Garuda.
Meursault2004, CC BY-SA 3.0 <http://creativecommons.org/licenses/by-sa/3.0/>, via Wikimedia Commons: https://commons.wikimedia.org/wiki/File:Taal_van_het_Adiparwa.jpg

If we were to take into account the ancient Malay records, we would find that Merong Mahawangsa was no ordinary man. His skills and talents were exceptional, but it was his lineage that many remembered. Although he called Rome his home, the warrior was said to have had roots that traced back to the illustrious Macedonian conqueror Alexander the Great.

With provisions stocked to the brim and the ships ready to combat the merciless tides of the Mediterranean Sea, Merong led the fleet to the horizon. The Romans disembarked at various regions and kingdoms along the way, perhaps to refill their supplies and repair the damage to their ships caused by the thunderous storms and waves. Each time they made a stop, the Romans were warmly welcomed by the locals, but news of the missing princess was nowhere to be heard. Days turned to weeks, and weeks turned to harsh months. Eventually, their voyage brought them to a region called Kuala Changgung (presumably somewhere on the northernmost part of the Malay Peninsula). There, misfortunes began to brew.

At first, the skies turned dark, with heavy clouds beginning to claim their spots in the heavens, covering the once bright sun. The silence was deafening. As a master of the sea, Merong could sense they were not alone. He turned to his men, ordering them to protect the Roman prince at all costs. Lightning bolts soon formed above them while sudden roars of thunder shook those who were less courageous. Amidst the dark clouds, Merong caught a glimpse of a massive shadow looming above their fleet. This shadow belonged to none other than the Garuda, who had arrived to stop the Romans' search for the princess.

A battle between the Roman fleets and the magical phoenix ensued. The Romans, undeterred by the terrifying look of the Garuda, launched their attacks without rest. Arrows and projectiles were shot in the creature's direction, yet the phoenix was able to deflect each one. The same could be said about the Romans. When the Garuda counterattacked, three of their ships faced significant destruction.

The battle went on for hours. The Roman fleets attempted to retreat, hoping they could disembark at the nearest port to repair and refill their resources. They eventually reached Kuala Parit (located in modern-day Kedah), yet the Garuda never lost sight of them. For days, the Romans were terrorized by the Garuda.

Once the battle cooled down, Merong Mahawangsa immediately voiced his plans to dock at yet another port to prepare themselves for another potential fight with the ruthless creature. However, the prince was too headstrong. He wanted to continue the search for the Chinese princess. Therefore, they went their separate ways. Merong planned to join the prince later as soon as his fleets were repaired and in a good enough condition to fight.

The prince's nightmare turned into reality. The Garuda managed to catch up with his fleets. Determined to kill the prince once and for all, the Garuda laid an assault that completely destroyed the ships. However, little did he know the prince survived. Holding on to a piece of a broken wood plank, he was carried away by the tides. Legend has it that the prince eventually reached Langkapuri, where he found the Chinese princess and married her.

As for Merong Mahawangsa, he kept his word. He set sail to find the prince, but to no avail. He did, however, stumble upon an island where he was warmly welcomed by the local inhabitants. Details are scarce, but it was believed that Merong Mahawangsa chose to stay on the island, where he laid the first foundations of an old Malay kingdom known as Langkasuka. He reigned over his new kingdom until he was called back to Rome.

Before he left, Merong passed the throne to one of his sons, Raja Merong Mahapudisat, who was tasked to expand the realm of Langkasuka. The rest of his children were also bestowed with different regions in the kingdom. His eldest son was crowned as the ruler of an unknown region in the Siamese Peninsula, another reigned over Perak, and his only daughter was given the land of Pattani.

The location of the Langkasuka Kingdom.
https://en.wikipedia.org/wiki/File:Langkasuka004.jpg

Throughout the years, Langkasuka (presumably modern-day Kedah) flourished under the reigns of Merong Mahawangsa's bloodline. The kingdom's influence experienced a decline during the 3rd century CE following the rise of Funan, a kingdom centered on the Mekong Delta. However, Langkasuka was able to get back on its feet when King Bhagadatta took the reins in the 6th century CE. By establishing relations with China in 515 CE, Langkasuka was said to have enjoyed a moment of prosperity-that was until they witnessed the rise of another powerful empire, Srivijaya.

Srivijaya, believed to have initially developed near Palembang in Sumatra, was an empire whose origins are steeped in both history and myth. The Kedukan Bukit inscription, one of the earliest records of the region, tells of a ruler named Dapunta Hyang Sri Jayanasa. He embarked on a sacred journey, a Siddhayatra, to expand his realm and assert his power. The significance of this journey is profound, representing a ritual of royal consecration and the divine endorsement of his military campaigns.

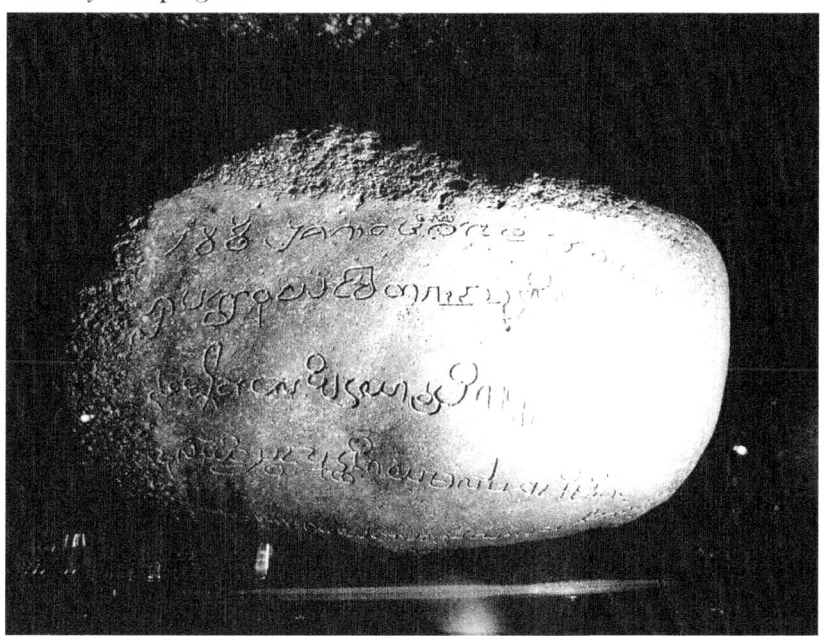

The Kedukan Bukit inscription.
Gunawan Kartapranata, CC BY-SA 4.0 <https://creativecommons.org/licenses/by-sa/4.0>, via Wikimedia Commons: https://commons.wikimedia.org/wiki/File:Prasasti_Kedukan_Bukit_3.jpg

Departing from Minanga Tamwan, the location of which is today's Minangkabau in West Sumatra, Dapunta Hyang set sail with a formidable contingent of twenty thousand soldiers. These troops, many of whom were the sea peoples or *orang laut*, played a pivotal role in establishing Srivijaya's reputation as a maritime power. Their first port of call was Matajap, an island possibly located in today's Vietnam or Borneo. Here, the empire began its expansion, demonstrating its military prowess and securing its influence over strategic maritime routes.

Dapunta Hyang's ambition soon turned toward Jambi, a region rich in gold that held a considerable reputation for wealth and influence. By subjugating Jambi, Srivijaya not only augmented its own wealth but also significantly enhanced its standing among the kingdoms of the region. The success against Jambi and other regional powers cemented Srivijaya's dominance, as it grew to encompass a network of Kedatuans, or local principalities, all pledging fealty to the central power in Palembang.

To maintain this allegiance and prevent rebellions, the Srivijayan ruler implemented a system of vassalage secured by the force of a sacred oath. The Telaga Batu inscription, found in eastern Palembang, is believed to have been used in such ceremonies. It warned of a curse that would befall anyone who dared betray the Srivijayan maharaja, ensuring loyalty through divine threat.

The late 7th century was a period of opportunity for Srivijaya, as it coincided with the decline of other significant kingdoms in the region, such as Tarumanagara in West Java and Kalingga in Central Java. Taking advantage of these shifts in power, Srivijaya expanded its control over crucial maritime routes, including the Straits of Malacca, the western Java Sea, and potentially even the Gulf of Thailand. By the end of the 8th century, the empire's influence had reached into western Java, with former kingdoms like Tarumanagara coming under its influence.

Srivijaya's prosperity was largely due to its strategic position, enabling control over the sea routes between India and China. The empire forged a tributary relationship with the Chinese dynasties, from the Tang to the Song, sending envoys to secure the favor of the Chinese court. Records of a Srivijayan mission to China in 1178 show the empire playing a crucial intermediary role in the trade of luxury goods, like the distinctive Bornean camphor, which was highly prized by the Chinese elite.

Srivijaya's influence did not stop there. Langkasuka eventually found itself absorbed into the ever-expanding Srivijaya Empire. Langkasuka, once a thriving kingdom in its own right, eventually became a tributary to Srivijaya. This did not merely mean submission; it was a complex relationship of mutual benefit. As a tributary state, Langkasuka enjoyed the protection and maritime prowess of Srivijaya and, in turn, contributed to the empire's wealth and prestige.

The thriving trade brought prosperity, as well as cultural and religious influences from other parts of Asia. The Hindu-Buddhist culture of Srivijaya permeated Langkasuka, as evidenced by archaeological finds that reflect the artistic and spiritual motifs common in Srivijayan culture. But perhaps more transformative was the gradual introduction of Islam, which was brought by Arab traders who frequented the Straits of Malacca, a region by then firmly under Srivijayan control.

These traders were not merely merchants trading silk and spices; they also traded ideas. Islam, which had already transformed much of the Arabian Peninsula and beyond, found fertile ground in the ports and cities of the Malay Archipelago. In Langkasuka, the ruling class began to adopt the new faith, a process that culminated with Phra Ong Mahawangsa, a descendant of the Merong Mahawangsa lineage, embracing Islam and laying the foundations for the first sultanate in Southeast Asia. In 1136, upon his conversion, he changed his name to Sultan Mudzaffar Shah I, becoming the first ruler of the Kedah Sultanate.

Chapter 2 - Adruja Wijayamala Singa: The Unsung Heroine of History

Similar to other old kingdoms and empires around the globe, Langkasuka was not free from the violent grasp of wars and invasions. By the 12th century, Langkasuka had spread its borders and covered several regions of the peninsula, from modern-day Perak all the way to the eastern coastal regions of Terengganu and Kelantan. While Hinduism continued to dominate the Malay Peninsula, the locals saw the emergence of Islam brought in by merchants hailing all the way from the distant lands of Arabia and India.

By the 13th century, the ruler of the Kingdom of Grahi (also known as Jawaka), which was an integral part of the greater Langkasuka empire, made a huge decision. Raja Sakranta was said to have converted to Islam, thus changing his name to Raja Zainuddin. Unfortunately, little is known about the Grahi king. He was believed to have abdicated his throne to his son Sang Tawal (also known by his Muslim name Sultan Muhammad) in 1267. The reason behind his decision was unknown, but certain sources claim Raja Zainuddin wished to focus his life on matters involving religion. Others, however, claim that the abdication was not done willingly. Since Islam, at the time, was not yet a popular religion, the king's conversion was not widely accepted among the subjects of Langkasuka. Hence, he stepped down and went on a journey across the archipelago, spending the remainder of his age spreading knowledge and ideas of Islam without a crown on his head.

Sang Tawal, on the other hand, only managed to enjoy a peaceful reign for several short years before chaos ensued. By 1279, the Sukhothai Kingdom of Thailand welcomed its third king of the Phra Ruang dynasty. Known in the history books as Ram Khamhaeng, the Thai king inherited a kingdom that was at its most prosperous. Apart from being credited for introducing the Thai alphabet, Ram Khamhaeng was also known for his military might. He managed to maintain a close relationship with the rulers of nearby city-states, but those beyond the Thai frontiers often encountered him in tense and violent confrontations. Even old records claim that his campaigns in Cambodia left the country utterly devastated.

Through the years, the Sukhothai king successfully expanded his realm, covering regions as far as Lampang (now the third-largest city in Thailand) to the Mon kingdoms in modern-day Myanmar and the Bay of Bengal. However, these territories were not enough to make Ram Khamhaeng sit still on his throne. With a highly capable army at his command, he turned his gaze south toward the Malay Peninsula.

Perhaps learning of the Sukhothai king's intentions, Sang Tawal quickly worked to strengthen his kingdom's borders. He ordered the construction of a fortress, hoping it could stop the Sukhothai army from infiltrating Grahi. But Ram Khamhaeng was not easily deterred. Campaigns were launched, and wars were eventually fought between the two rulers.

Days turned into months, and months turned into years, yet the two kingdoms never had a common ground. Sang Tawal was a formidable leader, but he alone could not win the war. Thankfully, the kingdom was blessed with another figure who would soon prove her might and surprise not only Sang Tawal and his high ministers but also the violent Ram Khamhaeng himself.

Known as Adruja Wijayamala Singa, this mighty female warrior was the daughter of Sang Tawal. Although raised as a royal princess, her curious spirit often took her beyond the safe walls of the palace. She yearned to experience the world and its challenges. From an early age, Adruja knew she must master the art of warfare should she ever be given a chance to govern her own kingdom. Hence, the princess spent her time not only in libraries and studies but also on the training grounds.

Before she reached her teen years, she could outpace boys her age in horse riding. Her skills in weapon play were also remarkable; even the most seasoned warriors nodded in approval at her talent.

As soon as she became a teenager, Adruja was allowed to follow her father into battles. She could often be seen carrying the proud flag of the Kingdom of Grahi, symbolizing its resilience and hope, whenever the king engaged the Sukhothai troops. When the battles ended, Adruja would rush to help the wounded warriors; she dressed their wounds and gave them water. By experiencing violent battles firsthand, Adruja became familiar with the brutal realities of war. The sounds of swords clashing, the sight of arrows in the sky, and the cries of fallen soldiers became a part of her life. However, not once did these experiences intimidate or break her. Instead, the princess gained a deep understanding of the cost of war and the value of peace.

However, peace was not yet an option for the Kingdom of Grahi. The Sukhothai troops showed no sign of retreat. They attacked helpless villages several times. Houses were burned, and families were slaughtered without mercy. Women who survived often were sexually abused by the brutal Sukhothai soldiers. Some were then killed, while others were spared, only to live the remainder of their lives filled with trauma. These sudden attacks undoubtedly saddened the princess, and the terrible fate of those women constantly kept her awake at night.

One day, the princess came up with the idea of establishing her own army made up entirely of women. In a world where women were only expected to spend their hours doing house chores and preparing meals, Adruja wished to prove that, like men, women too can participate in war and assist in putting the Sukhothai forces back to where they belong.

With eyes filled with hope and determination, Adruja proposed her plan to Sang Tawal. However, the king was rather skeptical of the idea. He claimed that women should never participate in such brutal encounters. Sang Tawal suggested to his daughter that she remain outside of the battlefield and limit her contribution to only mending the wounds of the soldiers. The Grahi king even suggested marriage as an alternative for Adruja. In his mind, by settling down with a noble prince or a brave warrior, Adruja would be kept away from the direct dangers of war, ensuring her safety and preserving the royal lineage.

Of course, Adruja immediately shut down her father's suggestions. She refused to marry and watch Grahi crumble from a distance when she could have played a greater part in protecting her people. She did agree to marry under one strict condition: the princess would only settle down with a man who could best her in a duel, fully knowing that no one stood the chance of even disarming her. Eventually, Sang Tawal relented to her wish the moment she recalled her bravery and experience of carrying and defending the kingdom's banner during several battles against the Sukhothai.

Finally getting her father's approval, Adruja left the palace almost immediately in search of capable women she could train to become ferocious warriors. She traveled to many villages, knocking on the doors of one house after another, but many refused to join her fight.

"Leave the fighting to our men. They are stronger than us." Most young women across the kingdom quickly shut the princess down.

The search was difficult. Eventually, Adruja encountered a group of widows who had lost their husbands to the violent wars against the Sukhothai army. They doubted the princess at first, but they finally agreed to participate after listening to Adruja's fiery speech. Adruja successfully recruited forty-one young widows into her special force, which she later named Seri Wijayamala.

The next step was to ready the supplies, weapons, and equipment for the force. The princess traveled to the port a short distance away from Grahi, where she purchased dozens of well-bred horses from the Arab and Turkish merchants. One particular horse caught her attention. Its coat was as white as snow, and its body was strong enough to withstand attacks on the battlefield. However, it was its exceptional speed that impressed the warrior princess. She made it her main steed and named it Halilintar (Malay word for lightning).

An example of a kelewang, which was used as a traditional weapon across the Malay Peninsula. *Tropenmuseum, part of the National Museum of World Cultures, CC BY-SA 3.0 <https://creativecommons.org/licenses/by-sa/3.0>, via Wikimedia Commons: https://commons.wikimedia.org/wiki/File:COLLECTIE_TROPENMUSEUM_Zwaard_in_sche de_-_RV-781-103.png*

Adruja also commissioned the production of special arrows that were said to be lighter and smaller than the usual ones yet could travel in the air faster and with extreme precision.

The women of Seri Wijayamala were expected to train all day long. They learned to ride horses, wield weapons, and fight like a true warrior. Most of them were masters of the bow and arrow, while others preferred the kelewang, a type of traditional single-edged sword capable of decapitating an enemy with a single slash. Even Adruja herself carried a kelewang named Kilatan (another Malay word for lightning or flash) into battle.

Done with the preparations and after countless hours of training, Adruja presented her special force to her father, Sang Tawal, and his ministers, who were, at the time, gathering around a map to strategize their next move against the Sukhothai. The ministers were quick to judge Adruja's forces. With skepticism clearly shown in their eyes, the ministers threw question after question at them, unconvinced that a troop full of widowed women had everything it took to go to war. Some even laughed at the sight of these women, which further infuriated Adruja.

Instead of answering the questions of whether or not her fighters could even wield a spear, the warrior princess ordered one of the women named Puspa to release an arrow toward one of the ministers. With extreme accuracy, the arrow flew and landed next to the minister, only an inch away from piercing his face. The atmosphere went quiet following this event; the ministers were stunned into silence. Adruja, on the other hand, went on to present herself before Sang Tawal and introduce her newly formed special force.

The Seri Wijayamala's training was finally put to the test when Adruja received news from a guard informing her of a sudden attack laid by the vicious Sukhothai at a village in the north. Without wasting another moment, Adruja and the Seri Wijayamala mounted their steeds and galloped to the village. Upon their arrival, they were greeted by an unimaginable sight of terror. Fires were blazing, burning homes to the ground. Children cried at the side of their father's corpses. Women were dragged and separated from their families. One particular Sukhothai soldier shoved a woman on the ground. As she lay helpless, the man prepared himself to violate her. This scene caused Adruja to run amok. She rushed toward the soldier and decapitated him using her kelewang.

As his head rolled on the ground, Adruja turned to her forces and ordered them to massacre the entire Sukhothai army.

It being their first time in a real battle, some of the female warriors puked the moment they witnessed dozens of decapitated heads and blood running endlessly on the scorched ground. Nonetheless, not one Sukhothai soldier survived. That night, Adruja and the Seri Wijayamala saved many women and children from dying at the hands of the unlawful soldiers.

However, the massacre eventually reached the ears of the Sukhothai king, Ram Khamhaeng. Vowing to get his revenge, the Thai king announced a full-fledged war against Grahi. He stated that he would lead a part of the Sukhothai troops.

Meanwhile, Sang Tawal, knowing that this battle would be nothing like he had experienced before, strictly ordered Adruja to remain within the city; perhaps, the king was worried about his daughter's safety. Adruja attempted to reason with her father but to no avail. She could only watch as Sang Tawal and the Grahi soldiers marched out of the city in the direction of the battlefield.

However, Sang Tawal did not know that Ram Khamhaeng was a cunning war strategist. The Thai king had split his forces into two: one was to meet Sang Tawal and his forces on the chosen battlefield, while another was to take the golden opportunity and breach the city of Grahi itself.

Thankfully, Puspa caught a glimpse of the Sukhothai forces from a distance as they approached the city. With haste, the warrior informed Adruja of the enemy sightings. Using the element of surprise (remember, the Sukhothai army thought the city had been left with only little to zero defense), Adruja and the Seri Wijayamala successfully destroyed the enemy and stopped them from entering the city.

Intent on participating in the war and defending her land, Adruja led her special force toward the battlefield where Sang Tawal was supposedly engaging with the other half of the Sukhothai army. As soon as she arrived, her nightmare turned into a reality: Sang Tawal and his forces were on the brink of defeat. Adruja charged into battle, immediately followed by the rest of her forces, who swiftly cut down any soldiers who stood in their way.

Puspa eventually managed to spot Ram Khamhaeng on his war elephant, which was trampling across the battlefield, injuring and killing

Sang Tawal's infantry. Alerted by Puspa, Adruja quickly shifted her focus and rode toward the Thai king. While doing so, she shouted an order to her archers to shoot Ram Khamhaeng's guards to create a path for her to get close to the king. It took only a few moments for the Seri Wijayamala archers to annihilate the royal guards. Then, a spear was thrown by one of the warriors, which pierced through Ram Khamhaeng. He immediately fell lifeless from his war elephant. Seizing the chance to end the battle, Adruja was said to have used her trusty kelewang to cut open the Thai king's torso until his intestines were visible. She then decapitated the king and showed his severed head to the remaining Sukhothai troops.

Consumed by terror, the Sukhothai troops surrendered. While Ram Khamhaeng's body was thrown into the sea, his severed head was kept in Grahi. It was not until a few months later that the head was returned to the Thai kingdom after a group of monks arrived to reclaim it.

However, Grahi was not meant to enjoy peace for too long. The kingdom would soon get attacked by Loe Thai, the new king of the Sukhothai Kingdom and the son of Ram Khamhaeng. Loe Thai swore to destroy Grahi and witness the Malay Peninsula burn. Unfortunately, not even Adruja and the Seri Wijayamala could stop the invasion. Grahi fell in 1325, and the region remains under Thailand's influence today.

With the defeat, Sang Tawal was left with no choice but to retreat. While he established another city known as Kota Mahligai (believed to be in the region of Bachok, Kelantan), Sang Tawal also gifted a piece of land to his daughter as a symbol of gratitude for her service and bravery. This particular land was known as Sekebun Bunga, and Adruja was made its very first ruler. Here, Adruja was better known by the locals as Cik Siti Wan Kembang—a name that was later used to refer to the future queens of Sekebun Bunga. Adruja ruled the region for a decade before passing away in 1345.

Chapter 3 - The Establishment of Melaka

Malaysia may appear rather tiny on the world map, but there is no doubt that the country has some of the most enthralling history and tales. Since the Malay Peninsula's history traces back thousands of years, it saw the birth of several powerful kingdoms and legendary heroes that have long been immortalized in various historical records. However, many agree that it was the establishment of Melaka (also spelled as Malacca) in the early 15th century that marked the beginning of Malaysia's golden age in trade and maritime power.

Although surviving records have different details of how exactly the kingdom was first founded, it is safe to assume that Melaka was the result of a series of intricate political maneuvers. Some may even agree that the establishment of Melaka is steeped in tales of not merely ambition but also betrayal and vendetta.

The story began with a man named Parameswara, the ruling monarch of Temasek, now modern-day Singapore. He was believed to have been a prominent ruler. His realm, bathed in prosperity and blessed with a bustling trade, excelled under his great leadership. Yet, it was his personal desire that eventually set in motion the wheels of change that would reshape the entire region.

Like many other governments of the old kingdoms, Parameswara did not oversee Temasek alone. He was often assisted by Sang Rajuna Tapa, one of his ministers who had significant influence. Aside from having a high position in the royal court, Sang Rajuna Tapa was also a father. His daughter was said to have been the epitome of beauty. Her looks and charms caught the attention of many, including Parameswara himself. Soon, the ruler of Temasek decided to take her as his wife, a decision that seemed romantic at first but would eventually become the start of a conflict.

The two were married on an unknown date, and from there on, Parameswara showered his newly wedded queen with affection and attention. However, like many monarchs of his time, Parameswara had several other concubines. Many of them were undoubtedly envious of the queen's beauty and the special treatment that she got. Later on, a few of the concubines grew to hate the queen to the point where they planned on turning Parameswara against her. They stirred a rumor that talked of her alleged infidelity. Not long after, the terrible rumor reached the Temasek king himself. Parameswara was an astute king, but his temper often clouded his better judgment.

Consumed by rage, Parameswara started an investigation to probe the claim's authenticity. He straightaway ordered a harsh punishment for his wife. Stories vary, but some suggest she was subjected to humiliation. The slandered queen was paraded in public without a thread of clothing on her body.

It is not known whether or not Parameswara regretted his rash decision, but we know that Rajuna Tapa refused to remain silent upon hearing news of his daughter's public humiliation. He was distraught and swore vengeance. He would do anything to ensure the monarch who had egregiously wronged his beloved daughter went down in flames. Without wasting another moment, Sang Rajuna Tapa came up with a plan. To ensure success, he sought help from the mightiest power in the region, the Majapahit Empire.

The Javanese Empire emerged in Southeast Asia sometime by the end of the 13th century. By the time Parameswara came to power, Majapahit had long expanded its wings. It was an expansive thalassocracy in the region that covered large parts of modern-day Indonesia and beyond. Its navy power was unparalleled, and its soldiers were known to never back down until they accomplished their mission. Majapahit's influence was absolutely impressive, and allying with such a force was wise on Sang Rajuna Tapa's part.

Ready to see Parameswara suffer, Sang Rajuna Tapa, along with a force sent by Majapahit, besieged Temasek. The siege was, of course, not a walk in the park, as the island was known for its formidable defenses that could withstand such an attack for quite some time. Nevertheless, no one should underestimate Majapahit's military prowess, and combined with Sang Rajuna Tapa's knowledge of the city's weak points, the city was bound to fall. Things came to a boil when Sang Rajuna Tapa, in a fateful act of betrayal and vengeance, successfully opened the city's gates to the fierce invaders.

As the Majapahit forces poured into the city, wreaking havoc, Parameswara sank to the floor. He realized that he would soon face his fate should he attempt to hold his ground. Thus, the Temasek king made a hasty retreat. He fled northward, heading toward the Malay Peninsula. However, Parameswara was not planning on leaving behind his life as a ruler. He made his way to the top yet again by founding what would later become one of the most influential sultanates in Southeast Asian history: Melaka.

Interestingly, the story of Parameswara's founding of Melaka does not rest on a singular narrative. Another popular and widely accepted version is recorded in the *Suma Oriental*, a 16th-century record authored by Tomé Pires, a Portuguese apothecary and colonial administrator. If we were to take account of Pires's records, the beginning of his narrative brings us to Palembang.

Palembang was once a great city in the heart of the Srivijaya Empire. Parameswara, at least according to Pires, was born in that city. However, by 1377, Southeast Asia witnessed a change in power. The Majapahit Empire was growing tremendously, and many felt its military prowess, especially Srivijaya. Not a second was delayed when Majapahit noticed the decline of Srivijaya. Campaigns were launched, and Srivijaya was successfully conquered. With it, Palembang fell and came under Javanese control.

Following the conquest, Parameswara, who was the prince of Palembang, was to be married to a princess of Majapahit in an effort to seal an alliance with the naval empire. A wedding ceremony was held, and the two royal figures were wed. It is unsure if Parameswara ever harbored any romantic feelings for his wife, but the prince never planned on forging a peaceful relationship with the Javanese rulers. He refused to pay any form of tribute to the Majapahit rulers to portray his outright defiance against the invaders.

Parameswara knew he could not overthrow Majapahit right there and then. So, he pulled in the reins and waited for a sign of a crack in the powerful empire. When it happened, Parameswara took the opportunity to publicly declare his decision to retaliate, hoping he could liberate Palembang from the tight grasp of Javanese rule. Word of his rebellion swiftly reached the ears of the Majapahit emperor, who, in turn, dispatched his mighty forces to suppress the insurrection.

The early signs of Majapahit's decline might have been written on the wall, but the empire's soldiers were still a force to be reckoned with. Parameswara, who had terribly underestimated the military might of Majapahit, was stunned by the empire's swift reaction. Overwhelmed, the Palembang prince had only one way to save his life for another day; he was forced to flee the very city he was born in.

His flight brought him to Temasek. Here, he was welcomed by Temagi, who was believed to be the representative ruler appointed by the Siamese Ayutthaya Kingdom. Parameswara saw another opportunity to rise back to his feet upon his arrival in Temasek. Again, he planned another rebellion. He learned his lesson not to announce it publicly. Instead, Parameswara sowed seeds of rebellion by whispering to Temagi. He convinced the ruler that he had what it took to rise against Ayutthaya and be free of the kingdom's watchful eyes. However, under unknown circumstances, perhaps suspecting Temagi's loyalty, Parameswara changed his plan. He murdered Temagi and claimed the throne of Temasek for himself.

Yet, fate had another path for him. Upon learning of Temagi's murder, the Ayutthaya Kingdom sent out its forces to face the new, self-proclaimed ruler. Again, history repeated itself. Parameswara was heavily outnumbered and, with limited resources, failed to hold his ground. So, he chose to flee. Parameswara and his most loyal followers made their way to the north. They stopped by the Muar River in Johor first before continuing their journey to the Bertam River (the modern-day Melaka River).

Here, Parameswara and his followers sought refuge at a fishing village that belonged to a seafaring group known as Orang Laut. The village was rather quiet; since it was nothing more than a simple fishing village, it remained safe from the fierce forces of the powerful empires at that time. Considered a safe haven from battles and sieges, the number of refugees seeking shelter in the village increased each year. By the beginning of the 15th century, the village was no longer quiet, as it had transformed into a bustling area filled with people of various backgrounds, beliefs, and religions, including Buddhists from the north, Hindus from Palembang, and Muslims all the way from Pasai. The settlement eventually transformed from a modest fishing village at the mouth of the Bertam River into the very first piece of Melaka.

So, why Melaka? Where did this name come from, and what exactly was the reason that led Parameswara to choose this particular spot as the center of his new kingdom? Legend has it that Parameswara witnessed an unusual incident while resting by the Bertam River. This tale involves a mouse deer and Parameswara's own hunting dog. After being cornered by the hunting dog, what seemed to be a timid mouse deer was expected to succumb to its fate. However, much to Parameswara's surprise, the mouse deer kicked his hunting dog into the river, allowing it to escape unscathed. Considering the event to be a good omen, Parameswara, who had been resting under a tree called Melaka when it happened, chose the location as a site for his new kingdom, christening it with the same name.

Work began soon after, and Parameswara oversaw it. During its early years, Melaka flourished into a buzzing trade port thanks to its strategic location at the crossroads of the major maritime routes connecting East and West. Nestled between the Malacca Straits, it offered a safe and convenient harbor for ships sailing not only from the archipelago of modern-day Indonesia but also from China and India. To ensure the safety of merchants sailing into Melaka, Parameswara employed the Orang Laut, whose exceptional naval skills were beneficial in eradicating threats from pirates.

Melaka was soon recognized as a new burgeoning nucleus of commerce and trade by grand courts of various mighty Asian empires, particularly that of the Ming dynasty of China. Sometime in 1405, just a few short years following its establishment, Melaka welcomed a special envoy, Yin Qing, who had been sent by the Yongle Emperor (r. 1402-1424) of the Ming dynasty. This was not the only time Melaka received such an honor; it was just the beginning of an era of friendship between Melaka and China.

A memorial rock for the disembarkation point of Admiral Zheng He in 1405.
Mrpresidentfaris, CC BY-SA 4.0 <https://creativecommons.org/licenses/by-sa/4.0>, via Wikimedia Commons:
https://commons.wikimedia.org/wiki/File:Disembarkation_point_of_Admiral_Zheng_He_in_1405.jpg

In 1407, the prosperous kingdom again received a friendly visit from a well-respected Chinese envoy. This time around, Melaka welcomed the arrival of Admiral Zheng He, one of history's greatest maritime explorers. He would visit Melaka six times in total, which clearly signified the importance of Melaka as a vital political ally and trading partner for the Ming dynasty. When it comes to economic benefits, these visits encouraged a wave of Chinese merchants to make Melaka their port of call. Within just a short span of time, these merchants established their trading bases in the city, making it a melting pot of not only commerce but also cultures.

Another crucial transformation took place during the reign of Raja Tengah, the third ruler of Melaka. When the city saw the arrival of a revered ulama named Saiyid Abdul Aziz, the people of Melaka were exposed to the teachings of Islam. This religion found a place in the hearts of nearly everyone, from the king to the senior officials and the common subjects. Raja Tengah, who was said to have been captivated by the ulama's teachings, embraced the Islamic faith. He changed his name to Muhammad Shah and began to adopt the title of sultan, ushering in a new era known in history as the Sultanate of Melaka.

Reforms were introduced so that Melaka's government aligned with Islamic principles. This transformation was not only limited to the royal court. Apart from championing its title as a thriving commercial hub,

Melaka also became a center for Islamic studies. Before long, the port was busy with merchants setting up bases and scholars who hailed from distant lands. They traded, engaged in invigorating discussions, and pursued a never-ending quest for knowledge. Even the Jawi script, which was heavily influenced by the Arabic alphabet, became a medium for written communication and documentation in the region. The sultan also never failed when it came to spreading the seeds of Islam. Dozens of Muslim missionaries or *da'i* were dispatched throughout the Malay Archipelago, including to Java, Borneo, and the Philippines.

Through this cultural and religious renaissance, the peninsula was able to further develop the Malay language, literature, and arts, with Classical Malay becoming the lingua franca of trade in maritime Southeast Asia. This golden era of Melaka no doubt paved the way for the "Malayization" of the peninsula, crystalizing the Malay identity that can be seen today.

Although Melaka was continuously thriving, it was not immune to external threats. The sultanate's main rivals were the northern Kingdom of Siam and the declining Majapahit Empire to the south. While Majapahit struggled to rival Melaka (the once-glorious empire eventually relinquished control over Indragiri, Jambi, Tungkal, and Siantan to Melaka later on), it was the Ayutthaya Kingdom that posed a more formidable challenge.

During the reign of Muzaffar Shah (the fifth sultan of Melaka), the threat from Ayutthaya became even more apparent. In 1446, a year following his coronation, the Siamese kingdom launched an attack on Melaka, aiming to conquer the region. However, Melaka had prepared for this moment. Brave forces, under the command of a man named Tun Perak, were rallied, and they successfully repelled the invasion attempt. Sultan Muzaffar Shah was said to have been beyond grateful and impressed with Tun Perak's leadership. Tun Perak was appointed as bendahara, a position comparable to that of a chief minister.

Despite their defeat, the Siamese kingdom was ready to retreat. Under King Borommatrailokkanat a decade later, the Ayutthaya hatched another plan to take over Melaka, this time wielding naval power. Tun Perak immediately made a move upon hearing of this imminent threat. The sultanate's naval defenses were cranked up to eleven, and an impregnable barricade was formed near Batu Pahat. With work on the defenses completed, Tun Perak and another valiant warrior named Tun

Hamzah (also known as Datuk Bongkok) led a fleet against the Siamese. The two powers engaged in a fierce naval battle, but the might of the Melaka navy proved insurmountable. Again, the invasion was repelled. The Siamese forces were chased to Singapore.

However, that was not the end of the threats that loomed over Melaka. In 1469, another unfortunate event took place. This time around, it involved the forces of the Vietnamese kingdom, Dai Viet, which ambushed and enslaved returning Melaka envoys. Since Dai Viet was a Chinese protectorate, Melaka avoided any form of counterattack. Instead, the sultanate reported the ambush to China in 1481. Since the event was already years old by that point, the Chinese emperor was not able to do anything about it besides sending a letter to the Vietnamese ruler to express his disappointment. The emperor also granted permission for Melaka to retaliate with violence should the Vietnamese launch another attack-an event that never happened ever again.

The diplomatic bond between Melaka and China kept strengthening, especially during the reign of Sultan Mansur Shah (sixth sultan of Melaka). According to the *Malay Annals*, the sultan entrusted his bendahara, Tun Perpatih Putih (who was also the brother of Tun Perak), with the task of delivering a diplomatic letter to the reigning emperor of China. The bendahara had a way with words. He described Sultan Mansur Shah's grandeur and his flourishing kingdom, which captivated the Ming emperor. The emperor sent his daughter, Hang Li Po, to marry the Melaka sultan.

The Chinese princess was said to have traveled to Melaka accompanied by her entourage of five hundred attendants. As a wedding gift, Sultan Mansur Shah gave his wife a hill known as Bukit Cina, which was then turned into their settlement. However, the existence of Hang Li Po remains a matter of debate due to the lack of concrete evidence.

Nevertheless, the deep diplomatic ties between Melaka and China were undeniable-Chinese influences in Melaka can still be observed today in the architecture, festivities, and traditions of the city.

Chapter 4 - The Legend of Hang Tuah

In history, it is common for dozens of figures to become legends, with tales of their brave heroics and feats being passed from one generation to another. Hang Tuah is a great example of a popular legend from Malaysian history. Hailing from Melaka, the warrior was believed to have played a prominent role during the golden age of the kingdom. Although his existence remains a hot topic of debate among scholars, many cannot deny that the narratives of Hang Tuah's adventures played a role in unifying the people of the Malay Peninsula under a shared cultural heritage and identity.

The themes of heroism, loyalty, and wisdom in these stories served as guiding principles for the old and young. Back then, these tales were an integral part of teaching the locals about the virtues of integrity and resilience in the face of adversity, hence defining their moral compass.

Although records that detail the stories of Hang Tuah's early life are scarce, it is safe to assume that he had a rather humble beginning. He was born in 1431 to Hang Mahmud, one of the many royal guards of the sultan, and Dang Merdu Wati, who served as a *dayang* or a maid of the palace. Even in his early years, Hang Tuah showed signs of natural prowess, especially in martial arts. He picked up *silat*, a traditional martial art popular in the Malay Archipelago, and was able to master it in just a matter of several weeks. However, in his eyes, knowledge knew no boundaries.

Along with four of his closest friends–Hang Kasturi, Hang Jebat, Hang Lekir, and Hang Lekiu–Hang Tuah set on a journey to find Sang Aria Putra, a highly esteemed martial guru who lived atop a mountain away from the busy towns and villages of Melaka. Under the guidance of Sang Aria Putra, the five boys were able to hone their skills in *silat* and master the knowledge of warriors and guards, known in Malay as *Ilmu Segala Parajurit dan Hulubalang*.

Following their studies, Hang Tuah and his four comrades were put to the test, which eventually became a stepping stone for them to enter the intricate world of politics and the sultan of Melaka's luxurious palace. This particular test took place in a certain village that had recently been attacked by a few men running amok. This chaos was heard by the bendahara, Tun Perak, who, along with his guards, went to the village to suppress the chaotic situation. Surprisingly, Tun Perak and his guards were immediately overwhelmed by the malicious men. Fortunately, Hang Tuah and his comrades were nearby to help. Without hesitation, they charged into the fray and showcased their extraordinary ferocity. The aggressors were driven away, and Tun Perak was saved.

Impressed by their act of bravery, Tun Perak decided to introduce the five young warriors to the reigning sultan, Mansur Shah. Upon listening to the story of how Tun Perak was saved, Sultan Mansur Shah extended his welcome to the five men. They were accepted into the royal court, with Hang Tuah receiving the esteemed title of laksamana (similar to an admiral) and entrusted with the sultan's protection.

His newfound position as laksamana was just the beginning to his tale. From there on, Hang Tuah was involved in numerous diplomatic endeavors, acting not only as the majesty's absolute protector but also as a mediator and royal messenger. His journey to Majapahit stands out as one of the most significant, as he was tasked to represent Sultan Mansur Shah in seeking the hand of Raden Galuh Cendera Kirana, the princess of the Majapahit Empire.

A bronze artwork depicting Hang Tuah.
Chainwit., CC BY-SA 4.0 <https://creativecommons.org/licenses/by-sa/4.0>, via Wikimedia Commons: https://commons.wikimedia.org/wiki/File:Hang_Tuah,_Muzium_Negara_-_cropped.jpg

Of course, Hang Tuah's adventure in Majapahit had its fair share of tribulations. The sultan and the princess were wed, but there was deception lurking in the shadows. During a banquet held by the Majapahit emperor (possibly Singhavikramavardhana) to celebrate the union of the two royal families, a scheme was carried out by the mahapatih (the military leader of the Majapahit Empire) in an effort to discredit Hang Tuah and the Melaka representatives.

The start of the banquet was joyous. The air was thick with anticipation as representatives from various regions mingled, accompanied by the melodic tunes of traditional music playing in the background. However, despite the talks and laughter, the atmosphere turned tense. The mahapatih had launched his secret plan. He ordered his men to spike the drinks offered to the Melaka representatives, causing them to go drunk. Miraculously, only Hang Tuah was unaffected by the drinks.

Then, a fierce warrior showed himself to the intoxicated guests. This warrior, known as Taming Sari, was loyal to the mahapatih. Thus, when he was ordered by the military leader to challenge Hang Tuah to a duel, he did so without question. The Majapahit emperor was against the idea, as he did not wish to have any commotion. He sent his men to disperse the situation to no avail. Hence, a fight was set in motion.

Hang Tuah lunged toward Taming Sari. He stabbed his opponent with a *keris* (a traditional curvy-bladed dagger) several times. Taming Sari easily parried Hang Tuah's advances. Hang Tuah was never known to yield too quickly, and he attacked without losing his breath, moving fluidly in every pivot, duck, and roll. Yet, every stab failed to hurt the Majapahit warrior. Eventually, Hang Tuah discovered that it was not Taming Sari's skill alone that protected him; it was actually his weapon. Taming Sari's keris (which he named after himself) was believed by many to have been magical; whoever possessed it would be granted invincibility, which was why every attack attempted by Hang Tuah failed to leave even the tiniest scratch on him. So, Hang Tuah devised an impromptu plan to disarm Taming Sari.

With Taming Sari's keris now in his possession, Hang Tuah stripped the Majapahit warrior of his magical protection. It was not long before Hang Tuah successfully pinned Taming Sari down, forcing the point of the keris deep into his opponent's flesh, which almost instantly killed him.

Hang Tuah's victory ceased the commotion at the banquet and cemented the relationship between the two kingdoms. The emperor of Majapahit even went to the extent of handing a few of his territories to the Sultanate of Melaka, while Hang Tuah, whose reputation skyrocketed, was rewarded with the magical keris, Taming Sari, which became his weapon in all battles and skirmishes.

Also during his journey in Majapahit, Hang Tuah took the opportunity to hunt for more knowledge. Informed by Sang Aria Putra years earlier that there was another martial guru who went by the name Sang Persanta Nala in Majapahit, Hang Tuah set on an adventure to search for him. Hang Tuah acquired the knowledge of wisdom and military tactics, which he undoubtedly valued to the end of his life, from

Sang Persanta.

Hang Tuah's bravery and tales of his travels in Majapahit spread in Melaka like a blazing wildfire. His stories became the subject of evening tales, and his name eventually became well known throughout the peninsula to the point that even children looked up to him, wishing to be exactly like the laksamana when they grew up. However, not everyone wished to see Hang Tuah prosper; some wished to harm him without having blood directly on their hands.

Among those who were envious of the laksamana's increasing popularity was Patih Kerma Wijaya, who was said to be an exiled minister from Lasem, Java. Perhaps overwhelmed by his own failure, Patih Kerma Wijaya refused to sit down and do nothing while Hang Tuah rose to power in the royal courts of Melaka. A cunning strategist, he began hatching a devious plan to destroy Hang Tuah's reputation. He gathered those who harbored jealousy toward the laksamana and began whispering to them about Hang Tuah's illicit affair with the sultan's favorite concubine.

This rumor reached the sultan, with a few dubious witnesses (probably sent by the envious Patih Kerma Wijaya) claiming that Hang Tuah was a traitor. Enraged and feeling betrayed, the sultan called for his bendahara. Without investigating the accusation, the sultan hastily voiced his decision to punish Hang Tuah by death. His execution was to be carried out by the bendahara. However, the bendahara, who suspected foul play in this matter, refused to do so. After all, Hang Tuah had always shown his loyalty to the kingdom and would put the sultan's life before himself. The bendahara talked the sultan into allowing Hang Tuah to travel to Inderapura (modern-day Pahang), where he could seek an opportunity to prove his innocence and regain the sultan's trust.

Upon his arrival in Inderapura, Hang Tuah wasted no time establishing contact with Bendahara Seri Buana, the father of Tun Teja, a woman whom the sultan had long had his eyes on. This was a golden opportunity; Hang Tuah was confident that should he successfully present Tun Teja before the sultan, he could be pardoned and freed from the slander. There was, however, a problem: Tun Teja was said to have been engaged to Megat Panji Alam, the prince of Terengganu.

Intent on returning to Melaka and clearing his name, Hang Tuah devised a rather tricky plot. He courted the princess himself. Tun Teja was initially reluctant, but Hang Tuah's charm and persistent effort to win her over eventually bore fruit. Little did she know that Hang Tuah's interest in her was not romantic but political. Nevertheless, Hang Tuah and Tun Teja went on to quietly set off on a voyage to Melaka. The sultan of Inderapura, who later discovered Hang Tuah's trick, dispatched a force to intercept the voyage. They were thwarted by Hang Tuah's strategic brilliance.

As soon as they arrived in Melaka, Tun Teja was paraded to the palace. However, much to her surprise, she was presented as a bride not to Hang Tuah but to the reigning sultan. Realizing Hang Tuah had tricked her, the princess resisted. Legend has it that Hang Tuah worked a magic on her that made her forget the love she had for him and accept the sultan as her husband.

Meanwhile, Megat Panji Alam of Terengganu rallied his army to attack Melaka for stealing his promised bride. He and his men were almost instantly squashed by the forces of Hang Jebat and Hang Kasturi, who had been dispatched by Hang Tuah. Without Megat Panji Alam, Inderapura was unable to form an alliance with Terengganu. Consumed by rage and disappointment, the sultan of Inderapura pronounced a death sentence on Tun Teja's entire family. Hang Tuah, on the other hand, received a rather positive outcome. He was pardoned and reinstated as laksamana.

Despite his unwavering loyalty, Hang Tuah was not yet clear from the dark clouds of conspiracy. Again, envious figures spun treacherous tales of his infidelity. The sultan again ordered his execution. But Hang Tuah was saved once more by the level-headed bendahara, who chose to hide Hang Tuah in a secluded region of Melaka, far from the eyes of those who wished to harm him.

While Hang Tuah remained in hiding, his position was given to Hang Jebat, who was entrusted with the legendary Taming Sari keris. However, Hang Jebat refused to blindly serve the sultan since he had ordered an unjust punishment of his closest comrade. Fueled by anger and bitterness, Hang Jebat chose to take a stand and embarked on a bloody revenge mission. He unleashed a chaotic rampage in the royal palace. The broken warrior laid waste to all who crossed his path. None was able to best him due to his possession of Taming Sari. The helpless sultan, who witnessed the bloodbath, finally came to the realization that he was plagued by his impulsive decision to punish his most loyal admiral.

As things continued to get out of hand, the bendahara revealed to the sultan that Hang Tuah was alive after all. Grateful, the sultan pardoned Hang Tuah and ordered his return. In his view, Hang Tuah was the only one who could resolve the chaos. He entrusted the warrior with the grave task of executing his dearest friend, Hang Jebat.

And so, their rivalries began, going from close companions to mortal enemies. Both were a mirror to the other: Hang Tuah, a symbol of utmost loyalty, and Hang Jebat, the emblem of righteous fury. They fought each other for seven days until Hang Tuah managed to finally reclaim the Taming Sari keris through another one of his cunning ruses. Now left vulnerable without the keris, Hang Jebat felt a surge of excruciating pain inflicted by a stab from his once-beloved friend.

However, Hang Jebat's fury ran deep. Despite his wounds, the warrior wreaked havoc across the city. Eventually, his rampage ended in Hang Tuah's house, where he tragically died in the embrace of his dear comrade. Before taking his last breath, Hang Jebat was said to have looked Hang Tuah straight in the eye while telling him to always choose justice over blind loyalty.

In the sultan's view, Hang Jebat was nothing more than a traitor. He was to be removed from history, with the sultan ordering the erasure of Hang Jebat's footsteps. First, his house was ordered to be completely destroyed. When the sultan learned the news of a lady named Dang Wangi having given birth to Hang Jebat's son, he decreed the innocent child's death. Hang Tuah valued loyalty above anything else, but he was not devoid of humanity. So, the laksamana secretly handed the child, later named Hang Nadim, to the bendahara, who raised him in Singapore.

Following this tragedy, Melaka settled down as the sultanate began to thrive once more. Merchants poured in, and Melaka continued to be the epicenter of trade and culture, with scholars bringing tales of lands far beyond the horizon.

During this prosperous era, Hang Tuah, now no longer the spry young man he was before, found a new calling. As the Melaka royal court opened its door wide to diplomatic missions, Hang Tuah chose to leave his warrior days behind and focus more on becoming a roving diplomat. With his eloquence and wisdom, he found himself on journeys to lands far beyond the frontiers of Melaka. The warrior made use of his brilliant skills in communication and negotiation. From the

Majapahit Empire to India, China, Ceylon, and even the distant lands of Egypt, Hang Tuah executed his duties well, presenting Melaka's affluence to foreign powers with an unmatched grace.

Later, Hang Tuah was dispatched on yet another quest for love on behalf of the eighth sultan of Melaka, Sultan Mahmud Shah. This time around, his target was Puteri Gunung Ledang, a princess of unparalleled beauty who dwelled on the majestic Gunung Ledang (Mount Ledang). Hang Tuah, accompanied by another figure named Tun Mamat, managed to safely reach Gunung Ledang and meet the princess. However, getting the princess to agree to the marriage was far from a walk in the park. She was not charmed by Hang Tuah's way of words, stating that she would only agree to marry the sultan if they were able to fulfill seven conditions: they were to build a silver bridge to Melaka to Gunung Ledang and a golden bridge connecting Gunung Ledang to Melaka, seven trays of mosquito hearts, seven trays of hearts gathered from germs, seven jars of virgins' tears, seven barrels of young betel nut juices, and a bowl of blood from the sultan's first son.

Seeing that it was impossible to fulfill the conditions, especially as the sultan refused to spill the blood of his son, Hang Tuah failed his quest, which was a rare occurrence in the history of his career. He was believed to have been so overwhelmed by this failure that he was hesitant to return to Melaka. Some claimed that he tossed his keris into the river, vowing to return to Melaka only if it resurfaced, which it never did.

Many barely saw Hang Tuah as the years passed. While a few suggested that the warrior participated in the fight against the Portuguese when they first approached Melaka, others whispered of his quiet retreat to Singapore, where he spent his twilight years in peace. His famed Taming Seri now rests in the possession of the sultan of Perak.

However, no one can actually determine the fate of the loyal laksamana. His tomb has never been confirmed; one can be found in Tanjung Kling, Melaka, but many believe it only symbolizes the spirit of Hang Tuah, with his true resting place remaining a mystery. Nevertheless, his intriguing tales of loyalty, bravery, and wisdom continue to inspire generations. Today, schools, streets, and institutions in Malaysia have been named after him, ensuring that his legacy remains alive.

Chapter 5 - Threats from Faraway Lands

Ever since the early 15th century, the Portuguese kept themselves busy building an empire. As their empire grew, the Portuguese became deeply interested in dominating the spice trade, which could not only bring their empire onto a higher platform in the eyes of the world but also reshape global commerce and geopolitics. So, they kept their eyes open, observing the world's most important trade routes and hoping that there would be a day when they could eventually make a move and conquer these regions.

Then came a new discovery in 1497 that stunned the European sphere. News arrived that famed Portuguese explorer Vasco da Gama had successfully led a voyage around the Cape of Good Hope. This was the beginning of a new era. The European merchants had long dreamed of the day when they no longer needed to travel the treacherous Silk Road. When a maritime route between Europe and Asia became a reality, they were overjoyed. Europe, especially Portugal, was undoubtedly poised for a new age of exploration and expansion.

First, they set their sights on Cochin, India, where a person could find one of the finest natural harbors in the world. Cochin was also located on the Malabar Coast, which was close to traditional maritime routes linking the West to Southeast Asia and the Far East. Cochin's strategic location, combined with its position as the focal point for the spice trade, made it the perfect stronghold for the Portuguese should they wish to establish their dominance in the Indian Ocean trade network. Thus, they embarked on an invasion quest. By 1503, Cochin had been successfully integrated into their growing global empire.

However, this was not enough for the Portuguese to hang up their weapons for good. Far into Southeast Asia stood another lucrative trading hub: Melaka. The Portuguese Empire took its first few steps of conquering Southeast Asia. In 1509, twenty Portuguese merchants were sent to Melaka. After being granted permission from Sultan Mahmud Shah to dock their ships, the Portuguese quickly used the time they had to set up trading posts alongside other international traders in the city.

The arrival of the Portuguese merchants and their rapid construction of trading posts soon raised eyebrows. Officials in the palace saw the sudden arrival of these foreigners as rather suspicious. The bendahara and the influential Gujarati merchants were the most vocal of all; they informed the sultan of their worry that these traders could be a threat to the kingdom. They demanded the sultan make a move, so he ordered a covert operation to be carried out in the dark of night. Disguised as merchant ships, a fleet of Melaka forces ambushed the unsuspecting Portuguese. This operation was a success, which led the Portuguese to beat a hasty retreat. The twenty merchants, who were still busy constructing their trading posts, were abandoned, resulting in their capture. However, rather than execute these Portuguese traders, Sultan Mahmud Shah imprisoned them—a decision that would soon contribute to the fall of the sultanate.

Meanwhile, a military genius named Afonso de Albuquerque had just made a name for himself. Albuquerque was a man of opportunity. As soon as he sniffed that internal strife and political instability were brewing within the Bijapur Sultanate, the admiral was quick to move his forces to Goa, where he planned on establishing a strategic foothold. Making use of the element of surprise, the Portuguese entered the city. The Bijapur sultan was able to muster enough forces to reclaim the city two months later, but the Portuguese soon made their appearance again. Albuquerque returned in November, this time accompanied by a reinforced fleet and troops.

Unfortunately for the Bijapur Sultanate, the Portuguese were absolutely a force to be reckoned with. With a combination of naval blockades, artillery bombardment, and land assaults, the Portuguese managed to overpower the city's defenses without heavy casualties. By

1510, Goa went on to become an important Portuguese maritime base in the East. With Goa secured, Albuquerque was able to focus on another challenge.

In 1511, the admiral received an unexpected communication from a man named Rui de Araújo, one of the imprisoned Portuguese in Melaka. Through a series of letters, Albuquerque was fed invaluable information about Melaka, from the kingdom's population to the city's layout, military strength, and internal political issues. Many may wonder how exactly this prisoner was able to send letters across the vast Indian Ocean. The answer lies in Nina Chatu, the leader of the Tamil community in Melaka, who held a personal grudge against Sultan Mahmud Shah.

Sultan Mahmud Shah inherited the sultanate when his father, Sultan Alauddin Riayat Shah I, died in 1488. He was a young man when he rose to the throne, and presumably due to his age, Mahmud Shah was often criticized for his inexperience. The sultan was not everyone's favorite, and his reputation began to crumble further when he made a hasty decision to punish his bendahara, Tun Mutahir, who also happened to be the uncle of Nina Chatu. According to old records, Tun Mutahir was accused by the envious Laksamana Khoja Hassan of having been involved in a scheme to overthrow the sultan. Without substantial evidence, Tun Mutahir was charged with treason and put to death. Ever since that unfortunate event, Sultan Mahmud Shah began to slowly lose the support of his subjects, particularly those within the Tamil community and Chinese and Javanese traders.

Learning of the political turmoil and the sultan's weak position among his subjects from Rui de Araújo, Afonso, ever the opportunist, made a move. He moved his fleets from Cochin to Melaka in late April 1511, where he laid a naval blockade to prevent supplies from entering Melaka. Sultan Mahmud failed to lift the blockade because he lacked a military force at the time due to an ongoing war with the Hindu Aru Kingdom. Only a small local defense was dispatched, which was, unsurprisingly, no match for the larger Portuguese fleet. The blockade also put a strain on Melaka's food and supplies. The kingdom was put in a vulnerable position.

This was the right moment for Albuquerque to strike a negotiation with the sultanate. The admiral demanded the sultan return the twenty Portuguese prisoners. In return, he would lift the blockade. Sultan

Mahmud delayed his decision initially, hoping he could bide his time until his main fleet returned. However, the sultan was pressured by the Portuguese, who, by the middle of July, began bombarding the city. The sultan eventually agreed, but Afonso broke his promise and refused to lift the blockade. Instead, he made two more audacious demands from the sultan: compensation for the suffering of the prisoners and permission for the Portuguese to build a fortress in Melaka. At this point, Albuquerque's intention was clear—Melaka was to be a Portuguese colony.

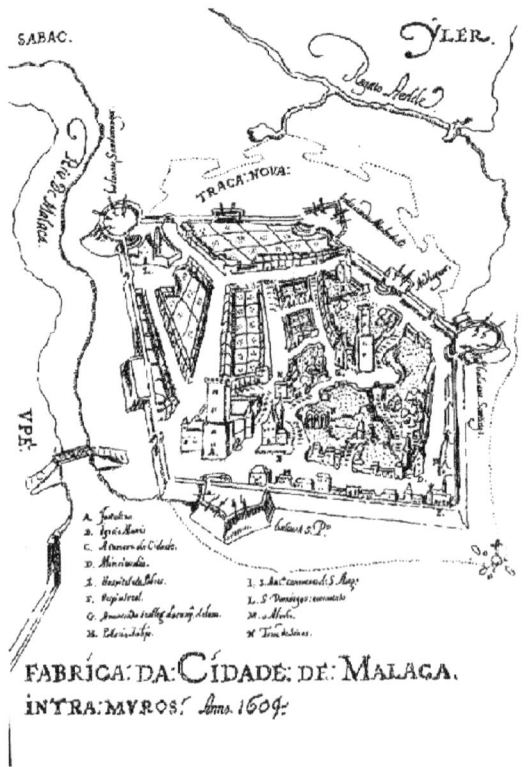

An illustration of the city of Melaka by Manuel Godinho de Erédia, a Portuguese writer.
https://commons.wikimedia.org/wiki/File:Malaca_(manuel_godinho_de_eredia_1604).jpg

And so, war was set in motion. With the help of Rui de Rojo, who was now freed, Afonso obtained information on Melaka's military strength. According to Rui de Rojo, the sultan had up to twenty thousand men at his disposal, though only four thousand of them were battle-ready at the time. These forces were primarily made up of Javanese, Persian, and Turkish mercenaries. They were accompanied by local Malay soldiers and dozens of war elephants. The Portuguese, on the other hand, had only one thousand soldiers, which included heavily armored infantry, riflemen, crossbowmen, and pikemen.

The Portuguese were outnumbered, but they planned on relying on their naval artillery. Thus, a strategic location was chosen. Thanks to Rui de Araújo, who pointed to the location, the Portuguese chose to assault the Melaka forces near a bridge connecting Upe, a commercial area located on the northern half of Melaka city, and the Royal Quarter. The Portuguese docked their ships by the side of the bridge so that they could make use of their naval artillery, which would bombard the incoming Melaka forces on land.

The Portuguese assault took place in two stages. The first phase, which began on July 25th, 1511, ended with the retreat of Sultan Mahmud, who fell from his war elephant while commanding his army. The Portuguese infantrymen were said to have used their pikes against the royal elephant, causing it to panic. The rest of the war elephants faced the same fate too—all of them turned away in panic and scattered out of formation. Although wounded, the sultan managed to escape with the help of his guards. Mahmud Shah's terrible state on the battlefield shattered the morale of his troops. The sultanate also lost foreign support. The Javanese withdrew their troops upon realizing that it was just a matter of time before the Portuguese would claim victory.

The first stage of the assault was called off when Albuquerque came to realize how short on provisions they were. Nevertheless, the invaders were able to burn the royal palace and multiple mosques along the way before leaving the battlefield.

The second phase took place in early August. Despite the sultan's impressive arsenal consisting of artillery pieces and firearms, they were not enough to repel the Portuguese army. By August 24th, 1511, the Melaka Sultanate saw its end, as Albuquerque and his men took full control of the city. Four hundred Portuguese soldiers poured into the city, marching to the sound of drums and trumpets. Those who dared to stand in their way were eliminated. The once-glorious city of Melaka was sacked. Its last sultan failed to defend his realm. He retreated to the mouth of the Muar River, where he set up camp.

Now a king without an empire, Sultan Mahmud Shah tried to muster a resistance from his new camp and attempted to reenter his former city after learning of Albuquerque's departure in January 1512. Yet, he failed once again. Forced to leave his encampment by the Muar River, the sultan retreated to Pahang. Here, the sultan survived an assassination attempt. Later on, Mahmud Shah journeyed to Bintan, an island kingdom southeast of Singapore. However, the sultan's arrival in Bintan was not a peaceful one. He managed to usurp the throne and once again waged war with the Portuguese in Melaka. But just as before, it resulted in failure. The Portuguese retaliated and wreaked havoc across Bintan in 1526 before returning the kingdom to its rightful ruler.

Finally, Mahmud Shah retreated to Kampar, Sumatra, and remained there until his death in 1527. His son, Alauddin, established the Sultanate of Johor, which, despite its sour relationship with the Portuguese, managed to eventually find a common ground with the empire, at least for a while.

As for the Portuguese in Melaka, their might would not go unchallenged for too long. They first experienced threats from the north, led by the ambitious ruler of Aceh, Sultan Alauddin Riayat Shah Sayyid al-Mukammal (not to be confused with the first sultan of Johor, Alauddin Riayat Shah II) over four decades later. Driven by the Pan-Islamic alliance in 1568, the Sultan of Aceh sought to expel the European invaders from not only Melaka but also from the coastal regions of India. With reinforcements sent by the Ottomans, the sultan of Aceh dispatched an impressive naval fleet to Melaka. They laid siege on the Portuguese-controlled city. However, Melaka's defenses had greatly improved, especially when it was put under the watchful eye of the seasoned commander Dom Leonis Pereira.

While the Sultanate of Aceh had the Ottomans as their key ally, the Portuguese were surprisingly supported by the sultan of Johor (Sultan Ali Jalla Abdul Jalil Shah II), who was not yet ready to face the implications of a shift in power. Together with forces sent by the Johor Sultanate, the Portuguese were able to put a stop to Alauddin's assault. But this was not the last of Aceh. The sultanate would continue to attack the European invaders. Johor would rekindle its friendship with Aceh and combine their forces against the Portuguese years later. Indeed, Melaka remained in the tight grasp of the Portuguese for more than a century, but these relentless assaults would eventually take a toll on their resources and influence.

By the 1570s, the Portuguese had been driven out of the Spice Islands by the sultan of Moluccas, resulting in the weakening of their influence over the lucrative spice trade. As they struggled with their waning dominance, especially in Southeast Asia, another formidable European contender soon rose, preparing to leave its mark on the region.

This other European power came all the way from the Netherlands. The Vereenigde Oostindische Compagnie (VOC), or the Dutch East India Company, was established in 1602 and was eagerly making its grand entrance into the global race for colonies and trade. With its exceptional fleets and resources, the VOC played a prominent role in shaping the geopolitics of Southeast Asia.

The VOC had its capital built in Batavia (modern-day Jakarta). Apart from serving as its primary base of operations where military campaigns, administrative affairs, and trade networks were managed, Batavia's strategic location also became a midpoint for the Dutch as they sought to control and profit from the immensely valuable spice trade flowing from the surrounding islands, notably the Moluccas.

Since they had their eyes on the Spice Islands, the Dutch acknowledged the importance of Melaka as the precious gateway between the wealthy islands of Indonesia and the markets of the Asian mainland. From the Dutch point of view, securing Melaka could boost their dominance in the flow of commerce in the region.

However, to get their hands on Melaka, the Dutch had to go through the Portuguese. Not deterred by their military might, the Dutch challenged Portuguese authority over Melaka. In May 1605, a fleet of eleven Dutch East India Company ships, led by Cornelis Matelief de Jonge, left the Netherlands en route to the Malay Peninsula. They stopped by Johor the following year and entered into negotiations with the sultan, hoping for a joint venture to topple the Portuguese. According to the pact, the Dutch would retain Melaka and be given the rights to trade in Johor. The Dutch promised never to wage war with Johor, and the two powers agreed to respect each other's religious practices and territorial autonomy.

With an alliance with the Johor Sultanate, the Dutch went on to besiege the Portuguese fortress in Melaka. The Dutch cut off any form of supplies from entering the city, hoping that hunger would engulf the Portuguese. Once the Portuguese were vulnerable, the Dutch planned to attack the enemy via a direct assault on land. However, there was a hiccup; Johor was not confident in the Dutch ability to take down the Portuguese. The sultanate only dispatched a few reinforcements to aid the Dutch. They did, however, provide a safe haven for the Dutch at their ports and granted them some supplies to keep the campaign running.

Without enough forces, the Dutch were not able to attack head-on. The Portuguese managed to hold their ground until August 1606, when a relief fleet from Goa under Dom Martim Afonso de Castro arrived. The confrontation between the two parties resumed, with a naval battle taking place off Cape Rachado. Perhaps luck was not yet on the Dutch side, as they were outmaneuvered by the Portuguese, resulting in their retreat to Johor. But the Dutch never planned on giving up. In the following years, other Dutch commanders, such as Pieter Willemsz Verhoeff in 1608, attempted to conquer Melaka, but these efforts failed.

A naval battle between the VOC fleet and the Portuguese.
https://commons.wikimedia.org/wiki/File:AMH-6473-
KB_Battle_for_Malacca_between_the_VOC_fleet_and_the_Portuguese,_1606.jpg

The turning point came in August 1639 when the Dutch returned with a considerable force from Batavia. They were also able to gain the allegiance of the ruler of Aceh despite his rivalry with the Johor sultan. The combined force laid siege to Melaka the following year. Both parties faced casualties, not due to each other's assault but to disease outbreaks. The death toll rose each day, taking the lives of infantrymen and skillful commanders. Yet, the Dutch refused to retreat.

The siege proved fruitful by November when famine terrorized the city. The Dutch and their allies pushed on, taking advantage of the dwindling Portuguese resources. Finally, on January 14th, 1641, 650 Dutch soldiers successfully stormed into the Portuguese citadel, marking the end of a century of Portuguese dominance over Melaka.

With the fall of the Portuguese in Melaka, the Dutch wasted no time to solidify their influence in the region. Trading agreements were made with multiple states across the Malay Peninsula, including Kedah and the state of Perak, which was famously known for its abundance of tin. These agreements showcased the Dutch intention to control the lucrative tin trade, an ambition that was not always met kindly. This was evident in 1651 when their outpost in Perak was destroyed and its garrison killed by the Malays.

Dutch Melaka, circa 1750.
https://commons.wikimedia.org/wiki/File:Malaca,_Malaka,_Histoire_g%C3%A9n%C3%A9rale_des_voyages,_Paris,_Didot,_1750.jpg

When Melaka was ruled by the Portuguese, the city was one of the most thriving trade hubs in Asia, second only to Goa. Yet, by the 1660s, Melaka's trade witnessed a decline under Dutch rule. This happened because of the Dutch, who valued Batavia more than Melaka. And so, recognizing the change, the Sultanate of Johor took the opportunity to open the seaport of Riau to unrestricted commerce. In the span of just a few decades, Riau's trade became a reflection of Melaka back when it was flourishing. The Dutch remained an ally to Johor, perhaps to avoid any unwanted chaos in the Straits of Malacca.

The 18th century saw the rise of the Bugis, a group from the southwestern region of Sulawesi who had migrated to Melaka following the Dutch conquest of Makassar. The Bugis successfully amassed enough forces to capture Riau and eventually the Sultanate of Johor in the 1720s. Under their leader, Daeng Kamboja, the Bugis laid siege to Dutch Melaka sometime in 1756. Fortunately for the Dutch, they received reinforcements from Batavia, which made it possible for them to turn the tide and force the Bugis to retreat.

The Bugis' dominance eventually waned as time passed by. Yet, the Dutch were not allowed to enjoy a moment of peace for too long. Later, another formidable shadow emerged from the horizon, their focus set on not only Melaka but also the entire region of the Malay Archipelago. The British Empire's colossal fleets were en route to Southeast Asia, prepared to challenge those who stood before them.

Chapter 6 - The Start of British Intervention

Britain had been expanding its reputation across the globe, but the heartbeat of its ambition in Asia was the British East India Company (EIC). Founded in 1600, the EIC started out with one aim: to trade in the Indian Ocean region. However, as the decades passed, its role changed from trading to administration, governance, and, at times, military intervention. Parts of India, for instance, fell to the EIC in 1757, with the company acting as a sovereign power on behalf of the British Crown.

Fast forward to slightly less than a decade after the EIC's invasion of India. The company saw another opportunity to broaden its wings. This time around, the British had their eyes on the Malay Peninsula, or what they called Malaya. Like many other foreign powers, Malaya's rich natural resources and strategic maritime location were irresistible.

The British entry into Malaya began in the late 18th century on Penang Island, which is located on the northwestern coast of the peninsula. The island's potential was recognized by a naval officer and private trader named Sir Francis Light in 1771. He envisioned Penang as not only a thriving trade center but also a powerful naval base that could greatly benefit the British. In 1786, Light launched a mission to get his hands on the region. However, he did not begin with aggression. Instead, Light entered into negotiations with Sultan Abdullah of Kedah, the reigning king of the region.

Francis Light knew he had the higher ground in the negotiations with the sultan, especially since he knew that the Sultanate of Kedah was in the midst of turbulence and uncertainty. Sultan Abdullah had found his realm trapped between the aggressive expansion campaigns of two colossal Asian powers at the time: the Siamese Kingdom to the north and the Burmese Empire to the northwest. The Burmese pursued territorial gains and were at odds with the Siamese following the sacking of Ayutthaya's capital in 1767. The Siamese, on the other hand, wished to assert their dominance over the northern Malay states so that they could create a buffer zone against the Burmese.

Sultan Abdullah desperately needed allies to save his territories from being invaded. Perhaps seeing the potential of revamping his defenses through an alliance with the British, the sultan considered Light's offer, which included a promise of military aid to repel any incoming foreign attacks along the coast. The sultan would also receive thirty thousand Spanish dollars annually in exchange for granting rights to the British to establish a trading post.

However, Light never intended to generously aid the sultan. In fact, his negotiation terms were not entirely transparent. He exaggerated the threats that loomed over Kedah to further pressure the sultan into considering his offer. Light promised Kedah military aid, but this particular term was ambiguous at best. Little did the sultan know that Francis Light had no clear directive from the EIC (at this time, he was not employed by the East India Company) or the British Crown to offer such assistance. Nevertheless, Light successfully convinced—or rather deceived—the sultan into agreeing to the negotiations. A treaty was signed between the two parties in August 1786, allowing Light to informally take possession of Penang. He named his newly acquired territory the Prince of Wales Island and established its capital, which he named George Town in honor of King George III.

The same year, the Siamese laid an assault against Pattani, which was at the time part of Malaya. Sultan Abdullah turned to the British for the military aid that Light had promised. Unfortunately, his call for help fell on deaf ears, and Pattani was lost to the Siamese. It is still a possession of Thailand today. Realizing that Light never intended to honor his promise of protection, the sultan rallied his army to drive the British out of Penang. The attack was supposed to take place at Seberang Perai, yet Francis Light was always a step ahead; he had already prepared a force to defend himself on the peninsula. The sultan's forces were forced to retreat.

As a result, Sultan Abdullah was left with no choice but to sign another treaty that allowed the British to formally take possession of Penang. The promised annual compensation of thirty thousand Spanish dollars had never been given. Instead, the British agreed to commit to an annual payment of six thousand Spanish dollars.

Francis Light's vision for Penang was not merely for military objectives. The British transformed the region from an uninhabited island into a buzzing trade hub. Traders and merchants flocked to Penang as soon as its port was declared duty-free. It was a hub of various cultures. Just as the century came to a close, its trade flourished with a diverse range of goods coming in and out of the island, from aromatic spices, including cloves and nutmeg from local plantations, to tea, ceramics, and pepper from Aceh, to vibrant textiles coming all the way from India.

However, Penang was not the only region that fell under the rule of the British; the island was merely the foundation for what would become a series of acquisitions, invasions, and treaties that led the British deeper into the peninsula's heartland.

With Penang Island secured, the British cast their gaze to the south. The British were well aware of the Dutch presence and dominance in Malaya's trade. They knew they were in need of yet another base in the region so that they could challenge the Dutch. In their eyes, Singapore was the perfect choice. Although it was nothing more than a humble fishing village at the time, its location at the crossroads of major maritime routes fit the needs of the British. To acquire this small yet precious island, the EIC sent out their visionary administrator and lieutenant governor Sir Stamford Raffles.

Raffles arrived in Singapore sometime in January 1819, when it was still under the control of the Sultanate of Johor. However, a golden opportunity shone in front of Raffles: the sultanate was currently embroiled in an internal affair involving a leadership scuffle between Sultan Abdul Rahman and his brother, Tengku Hussein. Since Tengku Hussein was the eldest, he was the rightful heir to the throne. But Tengku Hussein had been absent when their father, Sultan Mahmud Shah III, passed away, so the crown was given to Abdul Rahman.

Tengku Hussein was, of course, displeased with the situation. When Sultan Abdul Rahman's rule was acknowledged by the Dutch, Tengku

Hussein turned to the British, hoping they could aid him in reclaiming the throne.

Seizing the opportunity to intervene, Raffles announced his support for Tengku Hussein. However, his voice came with a price. A treaty was forged between the two parties that allowed the British to establish a trading post in Singapore. The British also agreed to pay an annual sum in return. Transforming Singapore into a busy trade hub, with Arab, Chinese, and Indian traders making it their pit stop, the British began to assert their dominance over the island by gradually limiting the power of the local rulers.

Of course, the Dutch were infuriated by this audacious move, viewing it as a breach of their sphere of influence. The two empires went on to have a contentious rivalry, each vying for more power and territories. They did not meet eye to eye for years, but the economic drain that came from their rivalry brought upon a much-needed resolution. In 1824, the British and the Dutch convened to sign the Anglo-Dutch Treaty, which redefined their colonial boundaries in Southeast Asia. Under the terms of this particular agreement, the Dutch acknowledged British rule over Singapore, while the British recognized Dutch control over Indonesia. The strategic port of Melaka was also passed to the British (ending the 183 years of Dutch occupation of the peninsula). In return, the British had to cede control of Bengkulu to the Dutch. While both powers bore the responsibility of eliminating the pirates harassing the region, the Dutch were no longer allowed to intervene in matters involving the Malay states.

With Melaka, Penang, and Singapore now added to their fold, the British had to streamline and formalize their administration. In 1826, all three of these crucial territories were unified as the Straits Settlements. Overseen by the EIC and later put under direct British control as a Crown colony in 1867, George Town was initially made the capital until 1832, when it was moved to Singapore. The Straits Settlements rapidly grew into major commercial hubs, leading to an unimaginable economic boom. From here on, the archipelago welcomed more immigrants from China and India, which gave birth to colorful multicultural communities. These immigrants brought with them not only their labor and skills, which were crucial to the economic expansion of the Straits Settlements, but also their customs, traditions, languages, and cuisines, most of which can still be seen in the region today.

With the blooming Straits Settlements, the British grew more interested in cementing their foothold on the peninsula. Malaya had a wealth of untapped resources, and in the eyes of the British, it would be absurd to ignore the opportunity to expand and capitalize on them. One particular resource that caught their attention was tin, which was experiencing a global demand in the 19th century.

The Malay states of Perak and Selangor, in particular, were rich in tin deposits, making them extremely valuable to the British. Tin mining also led to an influx of even more Chinese immigrants who were seeking an escape from either poverty or political turmoil in their homeland. Drawn by the allure of the "tin rush," Chinese immigrants began settling in the once quiet backwaters of Perak and Selangor, giving birth to many mining towns.

However, this rapid transformation was not without its complications. The Chinese immigrants formed different clans and secret societies, primarily for mutual protection and to stake their claim in the lucrative mining business. Rivalries became a common sight, and many erupted into bloody violence.

Perak was on the verge of chaos. In 1871, the state was plunged into trouble when the ruling sultan suddenly died. This immediately caused a power vacuum, with multiple contenders fighting to claim the throne. This political turmoil, combined with a series of wars between the Chinese secret societies (also known as the Larut Wars), drove Perak to face civil unrest. This unrelenting chaos was viewed by the British as both a challenge and an opportunity. They decided to intervene so that order and peace could once again be restored, but they also had another objective; this was the perfect moment to secure their economic foothold in Perak and oversee a steady flow of tin to meet global demands.

British intervention culminated in the Pangkor Treaty of 1874. Signed between Andrew Clarke, the governor of the Straits Settlements, and Raja Muda Abdullah, the son of the deceased sultan of Perak, the British successfully established their influence over Perak. While they recognized Raja Abdullah as the new ruler of Perak, the sultan had to welcome James W. W. Birch as his British Resident; he would assist in administration matters. Although framed as an advisor to the local sultan, Birch actually possessed significant power over state affairs, rendering the sultan a mere figurehead.

The Pangkor Treaty of 1874 might have quelled the civil unrest in Perak, but the growing British influence was clearly not accepted by many. After having a British Resident installed to eyeball their every movement and stripping their sultan of power, the locals chose to voice their outrage, with some getting involved in a few episodes of resistance. One of the most memorable rebellions against British control was led by a local chieftain named Dato' Maharaja Lela.

Dato' Maharaja Lela was not a stranger within the local Malay community. He was the chief of Pasir Salak and a staunch traditionalist who saw the installation of James W. W. Birch as a direct insult to Malay customs, traditions, and, of course, sovereignty. Birch was not a favorite among the locals. His series of reforms at modernizing Perak were seen as overbearing and insensitive to local sensibilities. He introduced policies that curtailed the powers of local chiefs. He was believed to have been extremely dismissive of local customs and traditions, frequently bypassing the traditional Malay elites in making decisions. Birch also attempted to control land ownership, which challenged the traditional Malay system of communal land rights.

The situation reached a boiling point in November 1875 when James Birch arrived in Pasir Salak to declare the British right to collect taxes from the lucrative mining industry. This was the last straw in the eyes of Dato' Maharaja Lela. It symbolized the erosion of Malay dignity and autonomy. Hence, the chieftain decided to take matters into his own hands. As Birch was taking a bath in the Perak River, Dato' Maharaja Lela and a few of his followers ambushed him. Caught by surprise, the British Resident could not do anything to defend himself. He was assassinated.

The sword used to assassinate James Birch.
Thomas Quine, CC BY 2.0 <https://creativecommons.org/licenses/by/2.0>, via Wikimedia Commons: https://commons.wikimedia.org/wiki/File:Sword_used_in_the_1875_assassination_of_J.W.W._Birch_(31839139523).jpg

News of the murder reached the British, who responded swiftly. A high bounty was placed on the head of Dato' Maharaja Lela and those involved in the assassination. They were eventually captured and put on trial in December 1876. About a week later, the chieftain was found guilty and punished to death. Dato' Maharaja Lela and his accomplices were hanged on January 20th, 1877.

This event marked a turning point in the British administration within Malaya. The British realized that it was necessary for them to establish a more centralized administration if they were to control and suppress local uprisings. So, another administrative structure was introduced. In 1896, the British established the Federated Malay States (FMS), which brought together four regions: the tin-wealthy states of Selangor and Perak, Negeri Sembilan, and Pahang.

The British saw the establishment of the FMS as both practical and strategic. Yet, in the viewpoint of the locals, it did nothing but further diminish and erode their local sovereignty. The Malay sultans only had a say in ceremonial and religious matters, while the British, in essence, gained complete control over the administration, the economy, and even the judiciary.

Because of this, the local populace grew even more angry. Dato' Maharaja Lela's resistance in the late 19th century might have ended badly, but his death did not scare or subdue the Malay communities. Colonial rule sowed seeds of nationalism and a desire for independence where local sultans and ministers held power.

Mat Kilau was another significant figure of resistance who bravely stood his ground in the hopes of protecting Malay rights and customs from being eroded by the colonizers. Mat Kilau was born in the mid-19th century to Imam Rasu, a well-respected religious leader, and his wife, Mahda. He operated mainly in Pahang. At the time of Mat Kilau's rise, the British were asserting their power in economic matters and also inserting their influence in religious and cultural issues among the locals. Although the British typically claimed to have adopted a policy of non-interference in religious matters, there were instances where colonial policies impacted religious institutions. Religious leaders who were seen as compliant would easily get the support of the British, while those who voiced their discontent would be treated unfairly.

So, a retaliation led by Mat Kilau began sometime in 1891. Known as the Pahang Rebellion (sometimes referred to as the Pahang War), the rebellion mainly involved guerilla warfare tactics, which made it difficult for the British to establish complete control over Pahang. From here on, the British, in their reports, often described Mat Kilau as a "rebel," but to many locals, he was a freedom fighter, defending Malay land and honor.

The British were able to quell the rebellion in 1895, with Mat Kilau believed to be among the warriors who fell during a battle with the British. His unfortunate death was said to have been reported by *The Strait Times* and *The Singapore Free Press* on October 22nd, 1895. However, Mat Kilau survived. Left with no choice but to self-exile, Mat Kilau moved from one place to another, living incognito for decades. No one was aware of his survival except for a few of his closest comrades, who brought that secret to their graves. Mat Kilau only emerged from hiding in 1969 (twelve years following Malaysia's independence), much to everyone's surprise, to tell the story of his life.

Then, as the 20th century came to a close, the British were met with another major resistance. This time around, the rebellion took place in Kelantan after the British, through the Anglo-Siamese Treaty, successfully took direct control of the state in 1909. Led by a leader famously known as Tok Janggut, the uprising in 1915 showed signs of success. After winninga battle against the British in Pasir Puteh (a district in Kelantan), Tok Janggut declared the district's independence. However, not everyone was pleased with Tok Janggut's rebellion, especially the reigning sultan of Kelantan, who saw his aggressive success as an act of defiance.

A portrait of Tok Janggut.
Divana AR, CC0, via Wikimedia Commons: https://commons.wikimedia.org/wiki/File:Tok-janggut.jpg

Branded as traitors, Tok Janggut and his followers were ordered to surrender. A bounty of $500 was placed on their heads. If they failed to submit themselves within seven days, the rebels would be charged with death. Despite this, Tok Janggut and his followers refused to surrender and hid in the jungle, waiting for another opportunity to free their beloved state from the clutches of the colonizers.

On June 25th, 1915, Tok Janggut led an attack on Pasir Puteh, along with a thousand of his most loyal followers, each armed with either guns or traditional weapons. Here, they were met with Indian troops dispatched by the British. Although Tok Janggut's forces easily outnumbered the enemy, the battle was won by the British, whose troops were better equipped. Tok Janggut was killed in the battle. While the bodies of the warriors were buried, Tok Janggut's corpse was paraded through Kota Bharu before being hung upside down along the shores as a warning for those who planned to go against the British.

These uprisings, although they ultimately failed to evict the British, highlighted the strong undercurrent of discontent within the Malay community. The stories of Dato' Maharaja Lela, Mat Kilau, and Tok Janggut were immortalized and became an inspiration for future generations in their fight for independence.

Yet, the journey to be free from these invaders was still a long one. The British would retain their tight grasp over the peninsula for several more decades.

Chapter 7 - The Struggles in Borneo

Similar to the eastern peninsula, the Southeast Asian island of Borneo had long been a focal point of regional powers that sought to gain a firm grip over the rich resources scattered throughout its dense rainforests and intricate river systems. The Sultanate of Brunei (established in the 14th century), for one, had expanded its dominion to control significant portions of Borneo, including the region known to us today as Sarawak.

The Bruneian Sultanate, as with other Malay Muslim kingdoms of its time, thrived on trade and were known for its naval might and diplomacy. Sarawak, which was somewhat loosely governed by the sultanate by the 18th century, was pretty much unknown to the outside world. Its abundant resources were largely untapped. However, things began to change in 1537 when Sarawak first appeared on maps drawn by curious European explorers, signaling the early stages of European interest in this particular region of Southeast Asia.

The discovery of antimony ore in the Sarawak River during the 19th century further boosted the region's popularity. Antimony, a lustrous gray metalloid, was used in alloys to increase hardness and strength. Therefore, it was not a surprise when the Europeans, who were experiencing the Industrial Revolution at the time, planned to sail across the ocean in the hopes they could get their hands on the valuable ore.

The Bruneian Sultanate also saw the potential for increased revenues, realizing it would be wise to tighten its grip on Sarawak. The sultanate made a move that would set in motion the early stages of British intervention in Sarawak. Oppressive taxes and controls were imposed by the sultanate, which eventually led to widespread discontent, especially among the Bidayuh and Malay communities. Weary of these overbearing policies and keen on self-governance without being closely watched by greedy outsiders, locals staged rebellions against the Bruneian Sultanate.

During these episodes of political unrest and economic opportunity, James Brooke, an Englishman with a penchant for adventure, entered the scene. Having purchased a 142-ton schooner with inheritance money from his father in 1836, Brooke dreamed of a grand exploration, both for scientific understanding and personal glory. Setting sail from Plymouth in 1838, he arrived in Kuching, Sarawak, in 1839.

Brooke's arrival was seen as a golden chance for the Brunei prince, Pengiran Muda Hashim (who was also the uncle of the reigning sultan of Brunei, Omar Ali Saifuddin II). Pengiran Muda Hashim wasted no time seeking Brooke's assistance. Much to the prince's disappointment, James Brooke did not immediately agree to the offer. He initially refused to intervene in Sarawak's internal affairs.

However, things changed a year later. Brooke was supposed to return to Europe, but he made the decision to stop by Sarawak for a second time before continuing his voyage. Seeing the state was still in turmoil, the Englishman changed his mind. He met with Pengiran Muda Hashim once more and set some conditions if he were to help. Perhaps in a dire need to quell the rebellion, the Bruneian prince agreed to fulfill Brooke's terms, which was to make him the governor of Sarawak.

A portrait of James Brooke.
https://commons.wikimedia.org/wiki/File:Sir_James_Brooke_(1847)_by_Francis_Grant.jpg

With his plans to return home now changed for the moment, Brooke provided crucial support to Pengiran Muda Hashim and successfully suppressed the chaos. Brooke's swift response greatly impressed the Bruneian prince. Grateful, Pengiran Muda Hashim signed a contract on September 24th, 1841, handing the title of governor of Sarawak to Brooke. Although Sultan Omar Ali Saifuddin II did not entirely favor the Englishman, he made Brooke's appointment official the following year. Brooke was crowned the first White Rajah of Sarawak in August 1842. This groundbreaking shift in power was symbolized by the hoisting of Sarawak's new flag in 1848, which bore the Brooke coat of arms.

The relationship between James Brooke and the sultan took a dark turn in 1844. Upon returning to Brunei after a significant absence, Pengiran Muda Hashim discovered that his position had been taken by his rival, Pengiran Muhammad Yusuf, due to a palace coup. With the support of James Brooke and British naval commander Sir Edward

Belcher, the Bruneian prince was able to reinstate his position and was even earmarked to succeed as the sultan of Brunei.

However, this reconfiguration of power did not sit well with many, especially with Sultan Omar Ali Saifuddin II and his own son, Pengiran Temenggong Anak Hashim. So, the two plotted an assassination of Pengiran Muda Hashim in early 1846, which was a success.

Pengiran Muda Hashim's brutal death undoubtedly infuriated James Brooke. In retaliation, the British, led by Rear Admiral Thomas Cochrane, stormed the city of Brunei later that year. Parts of the city were set on fire, forcing Sultan Omar Ali Saifuddin II to flee to Damuan.

Meanwhile, James Brooke's reign heralded transformative changes for Sarawak. Even before he managed to obtain the piece of land, Brooke had noticed the rampant piracy that plagued the region. Once in control, he moved swiftly to curb the issue. Administrative reforms were instituted, codified laws were introduced to streamline the justice system, and infrastructure projects, like roads and public buildings, were launched, forging a path for the state's modernization.

Word of Sarawak's transformation spread rapidly. By 1850, the United States recognized Sarawak as an independent state, with Britain following suit in 1863. But with rapid change often comes discontent. Not all were pleased with Brooke's reforms or his style of governance.

Among the most formidable opponents was Rentap, an Iban warrior chief from the uplands of the Sungai Sekarang. Rentap's disdain for Brooke's rule was mainly rooted in key policy changes. In his effort to modernize and consolidate power, Brooke aimed to eradicate the traditional collection of taxes by local chieftains. Perhaps to Brooke, these chieftains were akin to pirates, yet for many, this tax collection was a primary source of revenue. Furthermore, Brooke's interventions in Iban cultural practices, particularly headhunting rites, were seen as a direct offense to their way of life.

A relief representation of Rentap.
Benutzer D-M, CC BY-SA 3.0 DE <https://creativecommons.org/licenses/by-sa/3.0/de/deed.en>, via Wikimedia Commons: https://commons.wikimedia.org/wiki/File:Rentap.jpg

By 1853, Rentap had amassed a sizable force of brave warriors and launched an assault on the British outposts along Sungai Sekarang. The British were caught off guard by Rentap's men, leading to intense skirmishes between the two sides. In one notable encounter, one British ally named Alan Lee was slain by Rentap's son-in-law, Layang, with a spear, while another British man named William Brereton was seriously wounded, although he managed to escape. However, the British were not planning on retreating so easily. Brooke's forces were ordered to raze Rentap's base of operations, torching twenty longhouses (a type of traditional house in Sarawak).

In the wake of this destruction, Rentap relocated, constructing a new residence along the Sungai Lang farther upstream from Sungai Sekarang. This was the moment when he rallied his forces and shouted his famous phrase, "Agi Idup, Agi Ngelaban." which roughly translates to "We will fight as long as we live," before charging into another perilous battle.

However, the relentless pressure from Brooke's forces persisted. They eventually launched an attack on Rentap's longhouse, compelling him to retreat once more. Rentap then established another fortress atop Bukit Sadok, a hill that became synonymous with his story of resistance. The fortification of Bukit Sadok was further strengthened by a cannon known as the "Bujang Timpang Berang."

Brooke, recognizing the challenge posed by Rentap's stronghold on Bukit Sadok, initiated multiple attempts to capture the defiant Iban leader. It wasn't until 1861 that they finally managed to destroy the gates and breached Rentap's defenses on Bukit Sadok. They used several cannons, including one named "Bujang Sadok."

In the aftermath of the conquest, Brooke's forces razed Rentap's fortifications and dwellings on October 20th, 1861. Rentap, ever the resilient leader, retreated to Ulu Entabai, where he built another fortress. As he entered old age, Rentap and his followers moved once again to Bukit Sibau. It was here that Rentap's journey came to an end. A few years later, the great Iban leader passed away at the age of around seventy.

James Brooke kept a watchful eye over Sarawak until his death in 1868. Upon James Brooke's passing, his nephew, Charles Brooke, succeeded him. Charles continued his uncle's policies but also embarked on several initiatives of his own. Efforts were also made to expand the state's agricultural and mining sectors. Education became a focus, with more schools being established, thereby laying the foundation for a more literate and skilled population.

Charles was then succeeded by his son, Charles Vyner Brooke. During Vyner's rule, Sarawak witnessed significant sociopolitical changes. He introduced a constitution in 1941, which aimed at sharing administrative powers with Sarawakian representatives. This move was seen as a way to grant more autonomy to the people of Sarawak, which was completely different from the more autocratic governance of the past. However, the Brooke dynasty's plans for Sarawak took an unexpected turn with the onset of World War II.

While Sarawakians to this day remember Rentap as one of the unforgettable heroes who fought tirelessly for their land, Sabah (formerly known as North Borneo) had an almost similar chapter of history. This hero that the Sabahans immortalized was known as Mat Salleh.

To understand the roots of resistance in Sabah, it's essential to delve into the pre-British era. Sabah, like its neighbor in the south, had a surreal natural beauty and an unimaginable amount of valuable resources. Sabah was largely under the influence of the Brunei Sultanate. However, its eastern regions, owing to historical ties, were under the Sulu Sultanate. This duality in sovereignty made Sabah's geopolitical landscape rather complex.

The first significant foreign intervention in Sabah began in 1865 when the American Trading Company of Borneo attempted to establish a settlement on Pulau Balambangan (Balambangan Island). However, due to financial difficulties, the attempt was not realized. In 1872, a discerning British trader named Alfred Dent stepped in. Recognizing Sabah's potential, he negotiated with both the Sulu and Brunei Sultanates, which eventually led him to secure a lease for Sabah's territories. By 1875, this venture had evolved into the British North Borneo Provisional Association Limited.

In 1881, with significant contributions from William Clark Cowie, a notable shift occurred. The British North Borneo Chartered Company (BNBCC) was formed and was subsequently granted a royal charter. Seven years later, Sabah was declared a British protectorate. However, the administrative reins remained firmly in the hands of the BNBCC.

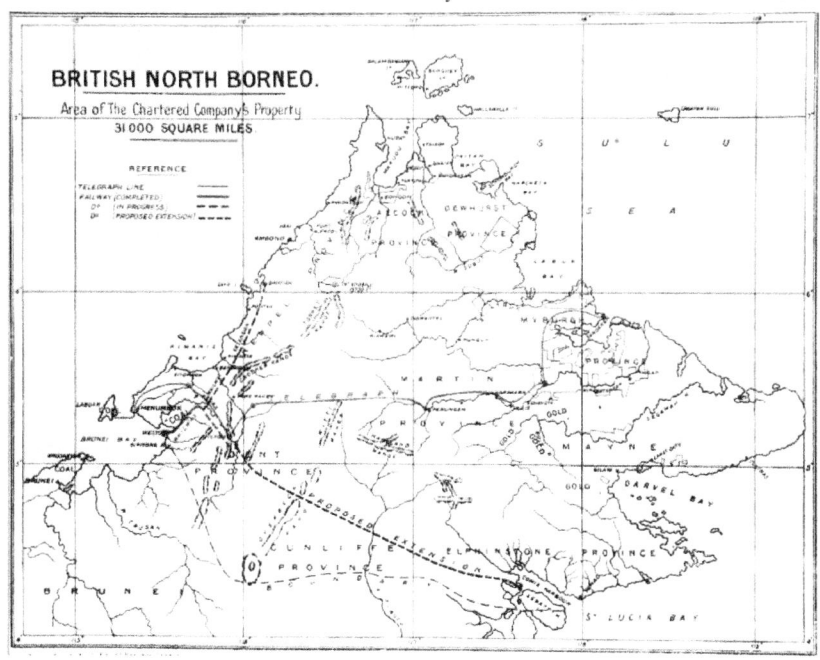

Area of the Chartered Company's Property.
https://commons.wikimedia.org/wiki/File:BritishNordBorneo-AreaOfTheCharteredCompanysProperty.PNG

Under BNBCC stewardship, Sabah underwent a transformation. The company initiated infrastructural developments, tapping into Sabah's rich resources. Trade ports emerged, railways were constructed, and vast expanses of land were converted to tobacco plantations, attracting Chinese migrant workers and creating a socioeconomic shift. Yet, not all was well.

Prior to British colonization, local leaders had the authority to collect taxes from their communities. However, with the onset of the British regime, especially under the aegis of the British North Borneo Chartered Company (BNBCC), a new taxation scheme was introduced.

To support their expansive projects, such as the railway line from Teluk Brunei (Brunei Bay) to Pelabuhan Cowie and the telegraph line from Labuan to Sandakan, the BNBCC imposed significantly higher taxes. These infrastructural endeavors, while aimed at modernizing Sabah and facilitating communication, came at a substantial cost, not just financial but also societal. To meet these developmental expenses, the people were burdened with higher taxes and exploited through a forced labor system. This atrocious system coerced locals into working on these projects without even providing them proper wages, let alone respectful treatment and rights.

One of the most problematic parts of this new taxation regime was the placement of a tax on daily necessities like rice. Rice, a staple in Sabahan diets, was now subject to an additional 5 percent tax. The Chinese community, which was greatly affected by the imposition, banded together to oppose it. Represented by the North Borneo Chinese Association in 1898, they sent a telegraph to London, pleading with the company to reconsider the exorbitant tax hike. Eventually, this tax issue became a rallying point for Mat Salleh and his followers. Rice was vital to them, as it was a key source of nutrition, and the British were not only taxing it but also humiliating the locals by using a few of them as tax collectors. These tax collectors took advantage of their newfound power and often overcharged, adding salt to the wounds of the aggrieved public.

The BNBCC implemented a mandatory boat licensing system, which only added to the discontent. Boats, essential for transportation and a lifeline for many Sabahans, now came under scrutiny. This licensing system was viewed as yet another oppressive rule, burdening the locals with more taxes. The Sabahans saw these policies as not just economically burdensome but also divisive; this was an attempt to fracture the unity of the Sabahan community. The combined effect of these tax practices fueled the flames of rebellion. This was where Datu Mohamed Salleh Datu Balu, often known as Mat Salleh, entered the history books.

Mat Salleh inherited his father's position as a high official in Sulu. His tale of resistance began after a certain event where two Dayak (another indigenous ethnic group in Sabah) merchants were brutally murdered by a few unknown villagers. News of these murders reached the British; the villager who delivered this news claimed the culprits were none other than the loyal followers of Mat Salleh. The villager also told the British that Mat Salleh had defied them by collecting taxes in Sungai Sugut (the Sugut River). Such claims were enough for the British to order Mat Salleh's capture. However, the warrior appeared before the British and, almost immediately, sternly defended himself with full confidence. Seeing no other choice, the British had to free him—at least for a while.

However, the warrior was not planning on walking away. Mat Salleh wanted to resolve the taxation issues and pressure the British to return power to the local chieftains. Mat Salleh initially took the step of approaching the British North Borneo Chartered Company with peaceful intentions. With a small group of followers, he addressed their issues, particularly the high taxes and the terrible treatment of the locals, to the governor of Beaufort, C. V. Creagh.

Unfortunately, Creagh was nowhere to be found when Mat Salleh arrived, as he had gone to visit Darvel Bay (also known as Lahad Datu Bay). Taking advantage of the governor's absence, the other British officials chose to ignore Mat Salleh and his followers. For two days, they waited for the British to respond, yet not a word arrived. Enraged by the terrible hospitality, they left without achieving what they had initially hoped for.

Once Creagh returned, the same British officials sent him a report, falsely claiming that Mat Salleh and his followers had assaulted them. Without investigating any further, Mat Salleh was once again put on a wanted poster.

The British dispatched a force to search for Mat Salleh and capture the defiant warrior. However, they failed to locate him, which led them to destroy Mat Salleh's home and his town. All of his possessions were seized. The British raised the stakes; they promised those who managed to get their hands on Mat Salleh a handsome payment.

This marked the beginning of an armed resistance. The first episode of the rebellion ended with the British destroying two of Mat Salleh's fortresses in Sungai Libawan and Sungai Sugut. However, Mat Salleh was able to retreat. On February 23rd, 1897, the British laid an assault on Ranau, hoping they could finally get their hands on the cunning resistance leaders. But, again, they failed.

The first display of Mat Salleh's armed opposition against the BNBCC occurred in July 1897. Mat Salleh, along with his followers, stormed and razed several houses, stalls, shops, and the company's administrative offices on Pulau Gaya (Gaya Island). Later that year, in a more significant show of defiance, he attacked and set ablaze the company's residency office in Ambong before retreating to Ranau. In December 1897, the British retaliated by launching an attack on Mat Salleh's stronghold in Ranau. This military expedition ended in disaster for the British, with many of their soldiers meeting their end at the hands of Mat Salleh's forces. Undeterred, in January 1898, the British, bolstering their forces, mounted another assault on Ranau. Facing this overwhelming might, Mat Salleh strategically retreated once again.

Tired of the chase, the BNBCC chose to sheathe their weapons and offered a peace negotiation with Mat Salleh. Although peace was agreed by both sides, the British were not planning on sticking to their words. Enraged, Mat Salleh resumed his resistance efforts.

The last confrontation took place in Tambunan, where Mat Salleh had meticulously constructed yet another fortress. This fortress in Tambunan was a marvel of guerrilla warfare design. Built using bricks, wood, and bamboo, it was virtually bulletproof. Each corner was heavily guarded, and the fort was riddled with secret tunnels and underground passages. These clandestine routes served dual purposes: facilitating the import of arms, food, and other supplies and offering escape routes when besieged by the enemy.

However, the tides of war are unpredictable. After a while, the British proposed a truce. Mat Salleh, despite objections from his men, agreed, hoping for a lasting peace. But this tranquility was short-lived. In 1899, the company made a move to seize Tambunan from Mat Salleh, reigniting the flames of war.

The culmination of this resistance came on February 1st, 1900. Mat Salleh's fortress in Tambunan faced an intense assault from the company. Despite their valiant defense, the fortress at Teboh in Tambunan fell. This marked the end of Mat Salleh's resistance. While his fate remains unknown, the British were able to cement their influence over Sabah for years to come.

British control over Sabah was interrupted when Japanese forces occupied the region during World War II. Yet, after the war, following the Japanese withdrawal, Sabah once again found itself under British dominion until its eventual merger into Malaysia.

Chapter 8 - The Japanese Invasion

The 1930s saw the rise of Japan, which had been rapidly expanding its influence in Asia. Motivated by both economic and geopolitical imperatives, the Japanese military made a daring step in 1931. They seized the region of Manchuria from China, shocking the international world and laying bare Tokyo's aggressive imperial ambitions. With the region now firmly in their grasp, the Japanese wasted no time in establishing Manchukuo, a puppet state that remained under Japanese rule. This, however, was only the beginning. The world watched, mostly in silence, as Japan gradually strengthened its grip on the region.

By 1937, relations between Japan and China had deteriorated to the point of full-scale war. The Sino-Japanese War highlighted Japan's insatiable need for natural resources. Battles raged, and territories were gained, but the war was about resources as much as it was about territorial domination for Japan. Oil, rubber, and tin were in great demand, as they were vital for Japan's war machine and economic sustenance. The late 1930s and early 1940s were defined by a rising sun in the East. Japan's grand ambition to establish a dominant presence in Asia was clear and undisputed. However, as Japan's borders grew, primarily in China and subsequently in Indochina, it sparked international alarm, particularly among Western nations.

In response to Japan's aggressive maneuverings in China and Indochina, the United States, a worldwide power with strong interests in the area, began taking steps to limit its rising supremacy. By 1940, America had imposed economic sanctions on Japan, including a ban on the export of essential resources like iron ore, scrap iron, and steel. The goal was rather simple: to crush Japan's industrial machine, thereby preventing its advance into neighboring territories.

However, the initial sanctions imposed by the US did not have the anticipated effect. Instead of discouraging Japan, the country appeared to be more determined in its expansionist ambitions. Taking into account the failure of the initial sanctions, the United States imposed even more severe measures in July 1941. It severed all trade connections with Japan and went as far as to freeze all Japanese assets under its authority. This caused a significant hit to the Japanese economy and worldwide trade.

However, the United States was not alone in its anti-Japan stance. Other major players, including the United Kingdom, China, and the Netherlands, joined the embargo bandwagon, putting restrictions on oil exports to Japan in response to similar concerns. Oil, a critical resource for Japan's military and industrial operations, became a scarce commodity. With these embargoes, Japan found itself in a precarious situation, deprived of the very resources that were crucial for its economic and military success.

Because of these challenges, Japan was standing at a crossroads. The empire could only think of a few options, though none of them were particularly appealing:

1. **Cease its imperialistic ventures:** This would entail Japan withdrawing from its acquired territories, particularly in China and Indochina. A move like this would be equivalent to a public declaration of failure.
2. **Maintain the status quo:** Without a significant shift in strategy, this approach would result in Japan's economy stagnating, if not regressing, as a result of the resource crunch.

While both options were completely different, the consequence was the same. Japan would "lose face"—an unacceptable result, especially since the Japanese valued their honor and reputation above all else.

However, there was a third option. It required extra effort, but it appeared to be the most viable given the circumstances. Japan could seek to establish its own economic sphere of influence, which was later dubbed the Greater East Asia Co-Prosperity Sphere (GEACPS). This ambitious plan entailed seizing control over parts of Southeast Asia, particularly the resource-rich Malay Peninsula.

To carry out this plan, the Japanese had to get rid of one obstacle in its way: the powerful US Navy stationed in the Pacific. The presence of the US fleet posed a significant threat; it had the ability to disrupt Japan's maritime routes, especially those in the East China Sea. These routes were key to unlocking Japan's ambitions, as they ensured the smooth transportation of resources gathered from captured territories back to the homeland.

The Japanese had to first neutralize this threat. So, Japan made the decision to launch a strike at the heart of the US Pacific Fleet. The main idea was to incapacitate the fleet so that the Japanese could buy the time it needed to expand its power in Southeast Asia and the Pacific without the interference of the Americans.

On December 7th, 1941, Japan launched its audacious attack on the US naval base at Pearl Harbor, Hawaii. Barely hours after the flames rose in Pearl Harbor, the Japanese troops were dispatched to another part of the globe. They made their presence felt at Kota Bharu (the capital of Kelantan) in the northeastern part of the Malay Peninsula. This was, indeed, the opening move in their Malayan campaign, and the suddenness of their operations definitely took the British defenders by surprise.

The Japanese employed a combination of tactics that were innovative for the time. The Malayan jungles were typically dense, so the British expected the Japanese to advance slowly. However, the Japanese had everything figured out. Instead of advancing by foot, they used bicycles and brought only light equipment. This allowed the troops to move with a speed that was unforeseen. Their mobility also allowed them to bypass, surround, and sometimes completely ignore strong British defensive positions.

The British had placed immense faith in their defensive strategies. The dense Malayan jungles were perceived to be a formidable natural barrier against any invader. But nature's barricade proved no match for Japan's innovative warfare. As the Japanese troops laid surprise attacks, outflanking and outmaneuvering the British at every turn, the British, along with their Indian, Australian, and Malay contingents, found themselves constantly on the back foot.

The British strategy, in many ways, was a series of underestimations. They had underestimated Japan's intent, its capabilities, and the speed with which its troops could move. This underpreparedness, combined with the unexpected tactics of the Japanese, made the British retreat, which became a recurring theme in the early stages of the campaign.

As the British forces were pushed back, Singapore became the final fortress, the last bastion of British resistance in the Malay Peninsula. This island, sometimes dubbed the "Gibraltar of the East," was believed to be an impregnable fortress, boasting vast naval bases, military installations, and a sizable garrison. However, its defenses were primarily sea-oriented. Since Singapore was surrounded by water, the British believed that an attack would come from the sea, not the land. But the Japanese, displaying their knack for unanticipated warfare, advanced down the Malay Peninsula and reached the narrow Straits of Johor in just slightly over two months following their arrival in northern Malaya.

British soldiers surrendering to the Japanese in Singapore.
https://commons.wikimedia.org/wiki/File:Bosbritsurrendergroup.jpg

The siege of Singapore was beyond intense. With aerial bombings, shelling from artillery across the strait, and ground pressure, the British and its allied troops found themselves trapped. The city's infrastructure crumbled, water supplies were threatened, and the morale of the defenders waned each day. On February 15th, 1942, having no other way to defeat the aggressive Japanese invaders, Lieutenant General Arthur Percival surrendered Singapore to the Japanese—a move that sent shockwaves through the British Empire. The British, who were eighty-five thousand men strong, were defeated by only thirty-five thousand Japanese troops.

Once they had established control, the Japanese did not waste a single moment to consolidate their occupation of the Malay Peninsula. The locals, especially the ethnic Chinese, were the ones who bore the brunt of Japanese aggression. The Japanese viewed the ethnic Chinese with deep suspicion due to their potential support for China in the ongoing Sino-Japanese War. As a result, massacres became the norm across the peninsula. Events like the Sook Ching massacre in February 1942 saw thousands of Chinese in Singapore rounded up under the pretext of anti-Japanese activities. They were interrogated, tortured, and killed, instilling fear and resentment among the local population.

Japanese soldiers shooting blindfolded Sikh prisoners.
https://commons.wikimedia.org/wiki/File:Japanese_shooting_blindfolded_Sikh_prisoners.jpg

Unsurprisingly, the Japanese were not just oppressive occupiers. They were also shrewd propagandists. They began to widely promote the concept of the Greater East Asia Co-Prosperity Sphere, portraying it as an unbreakable Asian brotherhood and a way to be united against cruel Western imperialism. The message was clear: Asia was for Asians. While this resonated with some, many viewed it with extreme skepticism, seeing through the facade and recognizing it as yet another form of imperialism.

Within this crucible of occupation and propaganda, Malaya saw the rise of the Malayan Communist Party (MCP), which had been around since the 1920s. Those involved in the party showed absolute commitment to resisting Japanese influence, yet it was their unwavering allegiance to communist principles that made them a wildcard in the eyes of many. Years back, the British had viewed the MCP with suspicion and often hostility due to its leftist ideologies. However, the British eventually changed their minds when the Japanese threat became more apparent.

And so, in a dramatic shift, the MCP was able to negotiate with British authorities, leading to the release of numerous left-wing political prisoners. These newly freed individuals proved instrumental in strengthening the backbone of the rising resistance. Realizing the potential of an organized local resistance against the Japanese, the British took it a step further. They established a training school in Singapore where MCP members could be taught guerilla tactics, sabotage techniques, and espionage. With this newfound knowledge and bolstered by British-provided weapons and intelligence, the MCP formally established a group known as the Malayan Peoples' Anti-Japanese Army (MPAJA).

Although the allegiance was not exactly expected, it was an alliance forged out of necessity, with both sides recognizing the mutual benefits. In the eyes of the British, the MPAJA could be a valuable tool to disrupt Japanese operations from the inside, potentially turning the tide of the war. Meanwhile, for the MPAJA, receiving the support of the British gave them an opportunity to chase the Japanese out of the region and solidify their own position in post-war Malaya, ensuring they would have a say in the future of the land they fought to liberate.

The MPAJA employed classic guerilla warfare tactics, making use of the dense Malayan jungles as their shield and cover. From hidden bases deep within the forest, they struck at Japanese supply lines, ambushed unaware patrols, and sabotaged various infrastructure. Railways, communication posts, and transport routes became frequent targets. The MPAJA sought to cripple the Japanese occupation and perhaps sow seeds of fear within their ranks.

However, the MPAJA's strength wasn't solely derived from their combat prowess. They built an intricate network of support among local communities. Villagers, many of whom had experienced Japanese brutality, especially the ethnic Chinese, provided the MPAJA with crucial intelligence, supplies, and shelter. This allowed the MPAJA to remain elusive and always one step ahead of the Japanese forces and their punitive expeditions.

However, the path of resistance was plagued with danger and risks. The Japanese were known for their brutal counter-insurgency measures. Villages suspected of supporting the MPAJA would often face severe consequences. The Kempeitai, the Japanese military police, conducted frequent raids, searching for MPAJA members and their sympathizers. Suspects were often subjected to torture and, worse, execution.

Yet, as the Japanese soon got embroiled in trouble with the MPAJA, Malaya once again saw a hint of light at the end of the tunnel. It was during this time that the MPAJA's role in post-war Malaya started to become a subject of contention. The British, having utilized the MPAJA as a tool against a common enemy, were wary of the communists' post-war ambitions. With the end of the Japanese threat, the MPAJA's communist ideology posed a potential challenge to the British.

As the sun set on the Japanese Empire, a new struggle was on the horizon. The MPAJA, emboldened by their wartime successes, soon discovered that liberating Malaya from one empire did not necessarily grant them a special seat at the table in shaping its future.

Chapter 9 - The End of the Japanese Occupation

As the final stages of World War II approached, the world was held in suspense, awaiting the conclusion of one of the most devastating conflicts in history. The war had sprawled across the globe, from the chilling battlefields of Europe to the tropical islands in Southeast Asia.

In May 1945, the world was shocked by the news of Germany's surrender, which signaled the end of Nazi dominance in Europe. Following their achievements in Europe, the Allied forces (a coalition led by Great Britain, the United States, and the Soviet Union) made a substantial shift to the Pacific, where the Japanese Empire (Japan was one of the three principal partners in the Axis alliance, alongside Germany and Italy) remained a formidable enemy, clinging tight to countries it had seized, especially Malaya.

The United States, specifically, had been pressuring the Japanese to agree to an unconditional surrender. The bombing of Tokyo in March 1945 was one of the many firebombing campaigns launched to push the Japanese to drop their weapons. However, despite the rising death tolls, Japan was not planning on giving up so easily. This was the moment that the United States made a crucial decision that would forever alter the course of history and hasten the conclusion of the war.

On August 6th, 1945, the United States dropped an atomic bomb, which they named Little Boy, on the Japanese city of Hiroshima. This was the very first use of nuclear weapons in warfare. The immediate impact of this bombing was undeniably apocalyptic for the Japanese. Hiroshima, once a bustling urban center, was annihilated in just a few moments. An estimated seventy-eight thousand people were killed instantly as a result of the explosion, which caused a firestorm that destroyed everything within its radius. Buildings were reduced to rubble, while people on the outskirts of the explosion received severe burns and injuries. The intense heat, which was hotter than the surface of the sun, melted glass and even stone.

Three days later, Nagasaki met a similar fate, though the geography of the city, with its hillier terrain, somewhat contained the blast's damage. Nonetheless, the explosion killed at least sixty thousand people. In both cities, those who survived the initial blast were left traumatized, facing a scorched landscape devoid of familiar landmarks.

The aftermath of the bombings was characterized by unimaginable suffering. Apart from the immediate casualties, tens of thousands more died in the subsequent weeks from injuries and the effects of radiation. This was a catastrophe for the Japanese and left Japan with little choice but to surrender. On August 15th, 1945, Emperor Hirohito announced Japan's unconditional surrender to the Allies, marking the conclusion of World War II.

While the bombings and the subsequent surrender dealt a heavy blow to the Japanese spirit and honor, casting a long shadow over the nation's post-war recovery, the surrender was viewed very differently in other parts of Asia. For the nations and territories that had suffered under Japanese occupation, the end of World War II was not only the end of a worldwide struggle but also the first light of dawn after a very long night.

Atomic bomb mushroom clouds over Hiroshima (left) and Nagasaki (right).
https://commons.wikimedia.org/wiki/File:Atomic_bombing_of_Japan.jpg

For the Malay Peninsula, the conclusion of the war did not instantly restore peace. As the Japanese forces withdrew, they left behind a power vacuum in the peninsula; there was no clear successor to restore law and order. The British, who had previously been Malaya's colonial masters, did not immediately reestablish their power. Possibly caught off guard by the suddenness of Japan's surrender, the British were preoccupied with internal matters. Because of their hesitancy, the doors were inadvertently left ajar, allowing a familiar local faction to seize power.

The MPAJA (Malayan Peoples' Anti-Japanese Army), which initially formed as a resistance movement against Japanese occupation, saw the window of opportunity and wasted no time plotting their moves to consolidate their control. Riding on anti-Japanese sentiment and bolstered by their contributions during the resistance against the Japanese occupation, the MPAJA expected a seamless transition into power. However, instead of being the heralds of peace and reconstruction, their short-lived rule became synonymous with violence and chaos.

With their newfound power, the MPAJA launched a ruthless campaign against anyone they saw as either sympathizers or collaborators with the Japanese regime. Throughout the campaign—or perhaps better worded as their pursuit of revenge—the MPAJA targeted members of the Kempeitai, police serving under the Japanese administration, who were predominantly Malays. The MPAJA's modus operandi was nothing short of horrific. Once captured, these former Kempeitai members were dragged to the dense forest, where they were then forced to dig their own graves. These unfortunate people were mercilessly beaten with wooden logs, metal rods, or the backs of hoes before being buried, possibly alive. There were some who faced a quicker death. Forced to kneel by the graves they had dug themselves, the MPAJA shot them at point blank. Some were sent to trial, but since they had no way of defending themselves, these former Kempeitai faced hangings. Those who attempted to intervene in this vicious punishment or even defend the accused were met with suspicion. Many remained quiet so they would not be labeled as traitors themselves.

The MPAJA's reign of terror didn't stop there. Their policies further alienated and infuriated the Malay community. They introduced regulations that enraged the locals, such as imposing exorbitant taxes on Batu Pahat residents regardless of ethnicity. Local communities were forced to hand over their harvests to the MPAJA. In many instances, their crops were looted and livestock taken without permission, which further infuriated villagers. The MPAJA also kidnapped young women, regardless of their marital status, so that they could either be incorporated into the communist ranks or used to reproduce their offspring.

Without any other power to stop them, the MPAJA could do anything they desired without having to face direct consequences. They could coerce locals into joining them, launch attacks on humble villages, or kill innocent civilians without reason. To add insult to injury, they even prohibited Muslims from congregational prayers, dismissively citing it as a waste of time.

Outrage and despair festered, especially among the Malays. However, things came to a boil with the rise of Panglima Salleh Selempang Merah, a local leader who refused to bow to the MPAJA's tyranny. He rallied his men and armed them with nothing more than just machetes and spears. Driven by their determination to see the end of the outrageous rule, this band of fighters launched daring assaults on several MPAJA fortresses. Under Panglima Salleh's leadership, they managed to suppress the MPAJA's influence, at least until the peninsula saw the arrival of the British.

Although they were not able to reassert their power instantly, the British were not ready to completely shift their focus away from Malaya. In fact, they had been planning for the administration of lands they would regain from the Japanese even before the end of World War II. Given the urgency of reestablishing power and restoring order, a military administration was regarded as the most efficient way for the British to accomplish their tasks.

The British Military Administration (BMA) was put in place in September 1945. Led by Admiral Lord Louis Mountbatten, the BMA's primary task was to disarm the Japanese troops and send them back to Japan. The BMA was also entrusted with the colossal task of restoring civil order, reconstructing infrastructure, and rehabilitating an economy ravaged by years of war and occupation.

Of course, the return of the British was not greeted with universal enthusiasm. While the Chinese and Indian communities, having suffered extensively under Japanese rule, were relatively more receptive, the Malays, emboldened by local leaders like Panglima Salleh Selempang Merah, were skeptical of renewed British control. Memories of pre-war British policies, which many Malays felt undermined their economic and political rights, still lingered in the air.

The reaction from the locals was clear, and the British were aware of it; after all, the peninsula had been through multiple invasions and much chaos. The British knew they had to do something to gain the trust of the locals. So, the BMA undertook several initiatives to reassert its dominance. One of the most important steps was to take action against the rampaging MPAJA. At this point in time, disbanding the MPAJA was of paramount importance, not only to the locals but also to the British; to restore order, they must prevent the rise of a powerful communist force in Malaya.

The British chose a rather diplomatic move at first. The British initiated discussions with MPAJA leaders. These talks were aimed at persuading the MPAJA to voluntarily disarm themselves in exchange for recognition and certain assurances. To sweeten the deal, the British offered monetary rewards to MPAJA members who agreed to put down their weapons. This "amnesty payment" was provided as an acknowledgment of their role during the Japanese occupation. This promise of financial compensation played a crucial role in persuading many rank-and-file members of the MPAJA to lay down their arms.

MPAJA leaders and members were also given assurances of safety, with some even handpicked to be integrated into the new administrative structure. The British were keen on using the experience of former MPAJA members for intelligence purposes, especially in countering communist insurgencies that could possibly emerge in the near future. However, while the British preferred a diplomatic solution, they did not shy away from displaying their military strength. The presence of the British Military Administration and reinforcements from British India acted as a deterrent, signaling to the MPAJA that any armed confrontation would be met with significant resistance.

The MPAJA marching during their disbandment ceremony in Johor Bahru.
https://commons.wikimedia.org/wiki/File:The_British_Reoccupation_of_Malaya_SE5878.jpg

The MPAJA was eventually dissolved on December 1st, 1945. Each member was given a sum of $350 and presented with a few options for them to live their lives. The disbanded members could pursue a civilian career or enlist in the police, local volunteer organizations, or the Malay Regiment. Over five thousand firearms were surrendered by 6,800 ex-guerrillas during demobilization ceremonies at various MPAJA headquarters across the nation.

Nonetheless, it was suspected that the MPAJA did not fully surrender their arsenal. The British, noting that most weapons turned over were older models, speculated that the MPAJA might have hidden newer firearms in the lush jungles. This suspicion was compounded when a British military patrol accidentally came across a well-armed Chinese community, which was apparently self-governing, complete with military training facilities and its own flag, during a raid at a former MPAJA camp. The very moment the Chinese saw the approaching British troops, they instantly engaged them, resulting in a conflict that killed one

Chinese citizen.

With the MPAJA disbanded, the BMA undertook several other efforts to revive Malaya's economy. Rubber plantations and tin mines that were previously abandoned or repurposed during the Japanese occupation were restored. Law and order were finally restored, putting an end to the extremely unjust punishments brought about by the MPAJA. To further regain the trust of the local populace, the British made the decision to reestablish the police force and judicial system. Policemen who had served under the Japanese, including those from the Jookidam, were often integrated into the new force after thorough vetting.

Acknowledging the ethnic tensions that rose during the war and skyrocketed under the fourteen-day MPAJA rule, the BMA sought to engage leaders from all ethnic communities in the governance process. This laid the groundwork for the multiracial alliances that later played a pivotal role in Malaya's journey to independence. Perhaps learning from their past mistakes, the BMA made efforts to address Malay worries, introducing policies that protected Malays' land rights and promoted their economic interests.

Nevertheless, the path was far from smooth. Communist insurgencies, primarily from remnants of the MPAJA and new communist factions, posed significant threats, which would eventually lead to yet another catastrophe in 1948 known as the Malayan Emergency. The British intervention also set the stage for the country's political evolution, as various ethnic groups began asserting their rights and envisioning a shared future.

Chapter 10 - The Federation of Malaya and the Communist Insurgency of the Malayan National Liberation Army

Another significant change took place across the peninsula as the world stepped into the year 1946. The British sought a more cohesive and centralized government to strengthen their hold on Malaya and address the difficulties of post-war reconstruction. This way, they could guarantee that the government was streamlined and that possible racial tensions, which had been on the rise since the departure of the Japanese, were resolved.

Therefore, Malaya was introduced to the Malayan Union, a unified administrative entity that comprised all the Malay states: Perlis, Kedah, Perak, Selangor, Negeri Sembilan, Johor, Pahang, Terengganu, Kelantan, and the previously British-administered Straits Settlements of Melaka and Penang. However, to realize the establishment of the Malayan Union, the British had to first obtain a positive nod from the sultans of each state.

This important task of securing the sultans' consent was assigned to Sir Harold MacMichael. The swiftness with which he managed to garner their approval has been a subject of much debate. The Malay rulers, having lived during the Japanese occupation, were vulnerable to accusations of collaborating with the occupying force. There are suggestions that the British used this as leverage. The rulers were also said to have been threatened with possible dethronement should they refuse to acknowledge the establishment of the union. So, they reluctantly gave their consent.

Of course, the establishment of this administrative entity was considered controversial by many, particularly the Malays. One of the Malayan Union's features that stirred the local populace was its citizen proposal. The British had attempted to implement *jus soli*, commonly known as birthright citizenship. By doing this, the British made it relatively easy for foreigners to acquire Malayan citizenship, which, of course, did not sit well with the Malays. However, because of strong opposition, this specific component of the union's agenda was never fully implemented.

A core feature of the Malayan Union was the transfer of power from the Malay sultans to the British monarchy. While the sultans maintained symbolic authority over religious matters, all other sovereign rights were ceded. A new phase of colonial rule began, as the Malayan Union was put under the jurisdiction of a British governor instead of a local ruler.

State councils in the former Federated Malay States were stripped of the limited autonomy they had once enjoyed. Instead, they functioned as an extension of the federal government in Kuala Lumpur, keeping themselves busy with minor local governance issues. The role of British Residents, who now superseded the sultans as heads of the state councils, signified a drastic decline in the political influence of the Malay rulers.

The Malayan Union also established the Supreme Court in the same year, appointing Harold Curwen Willan as the court's first and only chief justice. This court represented the highest judicial authority in the union, which further solidified British control of the peninsula.

The Malays protesting the establishment of the Malayan Union.
https://commons.wikimedia.org/wiki/File:Malayan_Union_protest.png

Yet, as Britain sought to tighten its grip over the region, a powerful Malay nationalist sentiment was brewing. Determined and driven by the erosion of Malay rights and the diminishing authority of their traditional rulers, one particular individual rose to become a key figure in voicing the Malays' concerns. This man was known as Dato' Onn bin. Jaafar.

Born into a family of Malay aristocrats and having served in various administrative roles under the British, Onn was deeply rooted in Malay traditions and politics. He was particularly alarmed by the perceived marginalization of the Malay community under the Malayan Union's policies. The union's propositions of equal citizenship rights for non-Malays and the reduction of the powers of the Malay sultans were seen as a threat to their historical and cultural identity. After the sultans lost their political rights, the Malays could be seen wearing white bands around their heads, a traditional symbol of mourning.

To champion the rights of the Malays and to ensure their political, cultural, and economic prominence never faded away, Dato' Onn founded the United Malays National Organisation (UMNO). Under Dato' Onn's leadership, the party rapidly gained traction, drawing members from diverse sections of the Malay community and galvanizing widespread support for its cause.

UMNO's strategy against the Malayan Union was characterized by civil disobedience. Members were said to have boycotted the installation ceremonies of British governors and refused to participate in meetings of the advisory councils. Malay participation in politics and bureaucracy essentially came to a complete halt.

The British, ever practical and sensing the shifting political winds, realized the untenability of the situation. The unwavering resistance rocked the foundations of the Malayan Union and made it clear that any administrative structure that ignored the feelings of the major races, particularly the Malays, was bound to fail.

So, the British sought to recalibrate their approach. Discussions were initiated with UMNO and other community leaders. These deliberations culminated in the dissolution of the Malayan Union and its replacement by the Federation of Malaya on February 1st, 1948.

It was undeniable that the Federation of Malaya differed significantly from its forerunner. While the Malayan Union had centralized authority, undermining the sultans' powers and providing equal citizenship rights irrespective of ethnicity, the Federation of Malaya restored the sovereign rights of the sultans in their respective states. To address the Malay concerns of an influx of non-Malay citizens, citizenship requirements were tightened.

The establishment of the Federation of Malaya marked a significant moment in the decolonization process. It laid the foundations for a more inclusive and representative form of governance, paving the way for Malaya's eventual journey to independence in 1957. However, it was still years before Malaya could finally be free. The road to independence was full of thorns, and another series of problems involving the Malayan Communist Party (MCP) would soon loom over the peninsula.

The Malayan Communist Party had contributed significantly to resisting the Japanese occupation during World War II. However, after the war, the MCP was not planning on holding back; they saw the return of British rule as a continuation of imperialist exploitation.

The MCP began its insurgency by establishing the Malayan National Liberation Army (MNLA), the armed wing of the party. The MNLA aimed to overthrow the British colonial administration and establish a communist state. Driven largely by ideological motivations, the MNLA exploited the rising ethnic tensions. Although the Malays were skeptical of this party despite their claim to fight for Malayan independence, many in the Chinese community felt otherwise. They were sympathetic to the MNLA's cause as they felt marginalized by pro-Malay policies. Knowing they could rally support, the MNLA embraced their portrayal as the vanguard of the Chinese working class, battling both colonial oppressors and the Malay elites.

Like the MPAJA during the Japanese occupation, the MNLA relied heavily on guerilla warfare. The countryside, with its jungles, provided an ideal backdrop for their campaigns. They were also masters when it came to terror tactics. The MNLA regularly employed fear to scare the public and prevent them from assisting the British. This included killing village chiefs, informants, and other people thought to be working with the British.

The MNLA grew bolder as time passed. They began a series of attacks on colonial assets. One of the most significant events that led to the declaration of the Malayan Emergency in 1948 was the killing of three European plantation managers in Sungai Siput, Perak. This audacious attack was a step too far for the British.

The British response was multi-faceted. They combined military action with socioeconomic reforms, aiming to cut off popular support for the communists. The Briggs Plan, named after British Army Director of Operations Sir Harold Briggs, is one of the most important strategies that the British launched. The main idea behind this forced resettlement plan was to relocate rural residents into supervised locations so that they could be kept away from the MNLA. Although they were safe from any harm inflicted by the MNLA members, many were discontent with this resettlement plan. Villagers were forced to leave their lands and settle in the "new villages," which were rather similar to concentration camps. Nonetheless, this strategy managed to prevent the MNLA from accessing vital resources like food, information, and potential new members.

To combat the MNLA's guerilla activities, the British carried out a scorched earth policy, which meant they destroyed any resources that could be useful to the guerrillas. Specialized military units were also established for intelligence gathering and direct engagement, while local Malayan forces were trained to create a local presence, making it harder for the MNLA to claim the conflict was purely colonial. Apart from guns and bombings, the British implemented psychological tactics, using broadcasts and leaflets to encourage MNLA members to surrender.

However, just like many other wars in history, both sides committed various atrocities during the conflict. The MNLA frequently targeted civilians in their operations. This was especially true for individuals they suspected of being informers or collaborators with the British. The aim of such attacks was twofold: to exact revenge and to send a clear message to the communities about the consequences of siding with the British forces. Such a climate of fear was exacerbated by reports of massacres in areas where the guerrillas believed the local populace had betrayed them.

The MNLA also often resorted to kidnappings, especially of influential figures like plantation managers and miners. These kidnappings served multiple purposes; they were used to establish authority over regions and to get ransom payments to further fund their operations. The guerrillas upheld a rigid code of conduct, and those who disobeyed MNLA orders or were considered traitors were frequently executed without any remorse. Booby traps, which also included improvised explosive devices (IEDs), were frequently used. Although the primary aim was to harm British patrols, the indiscriminate nature of such devices meant that civilian casualties were, sadly, not uncommon.

The British and their allied forces were known for the Batang Kali massacre, which was one of the darkest episodes during the Malayan Emergency. In December 1948, it was alleged that British troops from the Scots Guards separated men from their families in the village of Batang Kali for interrogation before executing twenty-four unarmed villagers using automatic weapons under the pretext they were insurgents. This incident has been the subject of much debate and several investigations, and it remains a contentious point in the history of the Malayan Emergency.

The massacre of Batang Kali was not the only time the British committed unlawful atrocities on the locals. Unthinkable torture, physical abuse, and degrading treatment, especially during interrogations, were common throughout the entire period of the Malayan Emergency (1948-1960). Headhunting, a practice common among the Ibans that the British had forbidden years ago, was revived. The British Commonwealth was said to have hired Iban headhunters to hunt for MNLA members or those suspected of collaborating with them. The intention behind this terror was crystal clear; they wanted to create an atmosphere of fear that would deter potential collaborators and obtain crucial information regarding MNLA operations.

Aerial bombings were also used to target MNLA hideouts. However, Malaya's deep jungles made it hard to accurately distinguish between MNLA camps and innocent civilian settlements. At times, this resulted in unintentional civilian casualties.

By the mid-1950s, the tide began to turn against the MCP. The British plans were working, and the rebels were losing strength. Noticing this, the government of the Federation of Malaya issued a declaration of amnesty to the communists in September 1955, offering them a chance to stop fighting and end the unnecessary bloodshed.

This led to the Baling Talks in December 1955. Held in the town of Baling, the talks saw Chin Peng, alongside two other MCP leaders, negotiate with Tunku Abdul Rahman, Malaya's chief minister; Tun Tan Cheng Lock, the founder of the Malaysian Chinese Association (MCA); and David Marshall, the chief minister of Singapore. During these talks, the communists sought legal recognition and the ability to participate in politics. However, their demands were dismissed, as the Malayan government was not planning on seeing communist activists regain influence in society. The talks ultimately failed to reach a consensus.

The Malayan Emergency continued for five more years and officially ended in 1960, although skirmishes continued in some places. By then, the MCP had been considerably weakened, both militarily and in terms of popular support. The combination of British military strategy, socioeconomic reforms, and the increasing promise of independence for Malaya had greatly eroded the MCP's base.

Chapter 11 - The Light at the End of the Tunnel

In the streets of Kuala Lumpur, Penang, and other major cities, there was a palpable sense of anticipation. The various ethnic groups—Malays, Chinese, Indians, and others—started to see the merit of putting aside their differences and working together. This burgeoning unity was not just a spontaneous sentiment among the general populace; it was also reflected in the strategic alliances being forged in the political arena. Leaders from the UMNO, MCA, and later the MIC began to recognize that their combined voices and united front would be the strongest weapon in their arsenal against colonial rule.

However, the path to independence was not universally uniform. Across Asia, countries under the colonial yoke employed various methods to shake off the chains that bound them. India, for instance, embarked on a tumultuous journey of civil disobedience against British rule, led by leaders like Mahatma Gandhi. Their nonviolent resistance, characterized by iconic events such as the Salt March, captured the world's attention and slowly eroded the British Empire's resolve. To the east, Indonesia confronted its colonizers, the Dutch, in a series of violent confrontations and diplomatic tussles. Their fiery passion for "Merdeka" ("freedom") culminated in a bitter armed struggle before sovereignty was finally recognized.

Yet, in contrast to the overt confrontations seen in India and Indonesia, Malaya's approach was markedly different. The leadership, while firm in their objectives, chose a path of negotiation and dialogue. This commitment to a peaceful transition was not born out of timidity but rather a strategic understanding of Malaya's unique sociopolitical fabric and the importance of maintaining harmony among its diverse communities. The logic was clear: a united Malaya, which spoke with one voice, was more likely to persuade the British to grant independence without bloodshed.

At the heart of this movement was a leader who would come to embody the spirit of Malayan independence: Tunku Abdul Rahman. Born into royalty but always a man of the people, Tunku was a visionary who saw beyond the divides of ethnicity and culture. He realized that for Malaya to truly flourish after independence, the nation needed to be built on the pillars of unity, mutual respect, and shared aspirations.

From his early days in the political arena, Tunku Abdul Rahman demonstrated an uncanny ability to bridge divides. He forged alliances with leaders from different ethnic backgrounds, a move that was both progressive and tactical. The foundations of this approach can be seen in the collaboration between **UMNO** (United Malays National Organisation), a primarily Malayan party led by Tunku, and the Malayan Chinese Association (**MCA**), which represented the Chinese community.

The initial establishment of this alliance was more than just political posturing; it was a pragmatic response to the British divide-and-rule strategy. Both parties realized that, singularly, their pleas for independence might fall on deaf ears, but together, their combined voice would be hard to ignore. This alliance marked the beginning of inter-ethnic cooperation in the political domain of Malaya, setting the stage for a united front against colonial rule.

The Baling Talks, though not directly related to the independence movement, had a profound impact on the **UMNO-MCA** alliance. The shared experience of navigating these talks and seeking a peace agreement with the communist insurgents further solidified their partnership. After the Baling Talks, there was a renewed sense of urgency. Leaders from both parties, spurred by the momentum from their combined efforts, became more vocal in their demand for broader representation in the governance of Malaya and a hastened drive toward independence.

However, for true representation, the alliance needed to encompass the voices of all of Malaya's major communities. Enter the Malayan

Indian Congress (MIC). Representing the significant Indian community in Malaya, the MIC was founded with a purpose parallel to its counterparts: voicing the concerns and aspirations of its community. The inclusion of MIC into the UMNO-MCA fold was not just a political move; it was also a statement of inclusivity, unity, and shared destiny.

V. T. Sambanthan, a key figure in the MIC, played a pivotal role in this union. A vocal advocate for the Indian community, Sambanthan recognized the merit of joining forces with the existing alliance, transforming it into what came to be known as the Alliance Party. His leadership, coupled with the efforts of Tunku and leaders from the MCA, ensured that the newly formed Alliance Party was more than the sum of its parts. It was a powerful embodiment of Malaya's collective aspiration for self-governance and independence.

In the run-up to the 1955 general election, the political climate in Malaya was electric. While a few smaller elections had been held prior, they served more as a learning curve, helping Malays understand the nuances of democratic processes and self-governance. These elections were significant, not just in terms of outcomes but also in the growing political awareness they instilled among the populace.

The first federal general election was held on July 27th, 1955. The contest was fierce, with multiple parties vying for influence. The Alliance Party, under the leadership of YTM Tunku Abdul Rahman, confidently fielded sixty-six candidates.[1] In contrast, Parti Negara, led by Dato' Onn Jaafar, fielded thirty-three candidates, and the Pan-Malaya Islamic Party (PAS) presented eleven candidates. Other contenders included the Labour Party, the Perak Progressive Party (which later became the People's Progressive Party), Pertubuhan Kebangsaan Perak, and Pertubuhan Melayu.

However, the limelight indisputably belonged to the Alliance Party. Their vision of a united, independent Malaya resonated deeply with the masses. Through rallies, speeches, and community outreach, they presented a dream of a nation where every community had a stake and every voice mattered. Their message was clear: together, as a united front, Malaya could step confidently into the future, free from colonial chains.

---

[1] YTM stands for "Yang Teramat Mulia," which is an honorific, almost similar to His or Her Royal Highness.

When the election results were announced, the Alliance Party celebrated a decisive victory. The coalition party secured a landslide victory by capturing fifty-one of the fifty-two contested seats. This overwhelming support, with over 80 percent of the voters backing the Alliance Party, underscored that their policies resonated deeply with the aspirations and demands of Malayan residents.

The Alliance Party's manifesto was both visionary and grounded. They voiced a bold promise: to secure independence for Malaya within four years. This commitment was not just a lofty ideal; it was also a calculated move. The Alliance Party leaders were confident in their negotiations with the British, having already established a rapport and having demonstrated their ability to maintain stability and unity in Malaya.

The Alliance Party was absolutely aware of Malaya's diverse fabric. They emphasized policies that ensured equal rights and opportunities for all ethnic groups. This focus on harmony and unity was both pragmatic and essential, considering past racial tensions exacerbated by the British divide-and-rule strategy.

Recognizing the power of education in nation-building, the Alliance Party promised reforms in the education sector. They aimed to create an inclusive education system where Malay, English, Chinese, and Tamil schools received fair support. Their commitment to ensuring compulsory education for all races demonstrated their dedication to an inclusive future.

Proposals like crafting a localized civil service and safeguarding human rights echoed the sentiments of a populace yearning for autonomy and justice. Moreover, their vow to protect the rights of the Malay rulers, emphasizing a constitutional monarchy, struck a balance between modern governance and cultural reverence. It was evident that this manifesto did more than just appeal to the electorate; it also captured their hearts.

In the aftermath of this overwhelming electoral victory, Tunku Abdul Rahman was inaugurated as the first-ever chief minister of the Federation of Malaya. On July 31st, 1955, with the approval of the British high commissioner, a new Cabinet was formed, marking a significant stride in Malaya's journey to autonomy and self-governance.

Following the formation of the new Cabinet, it was clear to Tunku Abdul Rahman and his colleagues that real independence would only be secured through direct and detailed negotiations with the British government. A historic trip to London was made in 1956, a journey that would significantly influence Malaya's trajectory.

Before embarking on this monumental expedition, the Malayan leaders indulged in rigorous preparations. They meticulously devised their strategy, underpinning their demands for independence with compelling arguments. They used their recent electoral victory to promote their mandate, as it signified the nation's readiness for self-rule.

The pursuit of independence culminated in a landmark conference at Lancaster House, London, named the Persidangan Malaya Merdeka, or Malaya Independence Conference. This monumental roundtable conference, held from January 18th to February 6th, 1956, spanned three weeks and was attended by representatives of the Alliance Party and the Malay rulers, alongside officials from the British Colonial Office.

The atmosphere was thick with anticipation. The British, with more than a century of vested interests in Malaya, both economic and strategic, were cautious. Yet, the Malayan leaders, bolstered by their electoral success and the global winds of decolonization, stood firm. They delved deep into various concerns, which included:

1. The future of Malaya within the British Commonwealth.
2. Financial affairs, administration, domestic security, defense, and foreign affairs, which would be under the purview of the Malay ministers.
3. The establishment of an independent commission to study and propose changes to the constitution without altering the special status of the Malay rulers.

Another pivotal component of these discussions was the formation of the Reid Commission. The British government, realizing the gravity of the situation, instituted this commission with the primary objective of drafting a constitution for an independent Malaya. Led by Lord William Reid, the commission comprised legal experts from both the British Commonwealth and Malaya. Their mandate was to ensure that the constitution would respect the diverse cultural and social tapestry of the nation while laying the groundwork for a modern democratic state.

As the negotiations continued, it became evident that both sides were converging on mutual terms. The British acknowledged that Malaya had showcased significant political maturity. However, they had conditions. Key among them was ensuring minority rights, preserving economic interests, and addressing the sultans' roles in this new nation. The Malayan leaders, while eager for independence, understood the importance of these terms and sought to address them in a manner that would benefit their burgeoning nation.

Finally, on February 8th, 1956, after exhaustive discussions, an agreement was reached. Malaya would be granted independence the following year. This moment was more than just a diplomatic success; it was also the realization of a dream nurtured over many decades.

The delegation's return home was nothing short of triumphant. As their plane touched down, thousands thronged to greet and celebrate the heroes who had secured their nation's future. The streets were alive with jubilation, with every cheer echoing the impending dawn of a new era for Malaya.

On August 31st, 1957, the Merdeka Stadium in Kuala Lumpur witnessed a ceremony that would forever be etched in history. Tunku Abdul Rahman, looking resplendent in his ceremonial attire known as the "Muscat Dress," delivered a speech that encapsulated the dreams of millions. Reflecting on past struggles and the promise of the future, he led the crowd in a resounding cry, shouting "Merdeka!" seven times. The most poignant moment of the ceremony was the lowering of the Union Jack at noon. The flag had fluttered over Malaya for over a century. As it descended, a new flag ascended in its place, its red and white stripes and blue rectangle with a crescent moon and an eleven-pointed star symbolizing a new beginning. It symbolized the birth of a new nation's identity.

And so, amidst joyous celebrations, the sun rose on an independent Malaya, marking the beginning of a new chapter of sovereignty, unity, and progress.

Chapter 12 - Post-Independence and the Establishment of Malaysia

Malaya found itself at the start of an entirely new expedition. With the buzz of "Merdeka" still lingering in the air, it was time to get in and handle the tasks of leading a nation. The Federation of Malaya was now a reality. It was a fresh nation with a mix of cultures and communities, all trying to sing the same national anthem in tune.

Malaya took the next step toward democracy in 1959 when the nation held its very first general election since its independence. The people spoke, and the Alliance Party, led by the popular Tunku Abdul Rahman, took the lead. Although writing a constitution that reflected the diverse mosaic of the Malayans was not a walk in the park, the government eventually succeeded in doing so. This new rulebook became the nation's guide on how to live together in peace.

However, peace would not be simply handed to them on a silver platter. The shadow of the Malayan Emergency, which started before independence with the communist insurgency, had not completely faded. Even after the Malayan Emergency officially ended in 1960, the threat hadn't vanished; it was just lurking around the corner. Malaya had to remain vigilant, countering insurgent activities to keep the peace and safeguard the fragile beginnings of the state.

As Malaya began to stand firmly on its feet, its leaders had an even bigger dream: creating a new country named Malaysia. This wasn't just about bringing a couple of places together; it was also about making a strong family out of different territories. The man behind this big idea was none other than Prime Minister Tunku Abdul Rahman. He believed that joining Malaya with the island territories of Sabah and Sarawak in Borneo, Singapore, and Brunei could make the region safer and help everyone make more money and live better.

Tunku's plan was not without its considerations. In 1962, the Cobbold Commission—named for its head, Lord Cobbold—was established in 1962 to address a few particular issues. One of the commission's most important assignments was to find out how the Borneo territories felt about joining Malaya and forming Malaysia. Members of the commission faced long travels and interviews with a broad range of the Sabah and Sarawakian populace. However, the efforts were definitely worth it. A sizable majority supported the merger, although they wanted certain conditions to protect regional identities and interests.

However, the path to unite Malaya's neighboring regions and establish Malaysia was not straightforward. The Philippines and neighboring Indonesia, both of which had stakes in the Borneo region, became interested in the formation of the new nation. To address potential regional conflicts, the leaders of Malaya, Indonesia, and the Philippines convened and eventually reached an agreement known as the Manila Accord. This agreement was crucial. Since it stated that the establishment of Malaysia would depend on the results of a United Nations assessment, it was the responsibility of the UN to guarantee that the people of Sarawak and Sabah genuinely embraced this new national identity.

That was one task down. Malaya was tested with another challenge, though. An internal struggle was brewing, adding complexity to the establishment of the nation. Prospective member states were cautious about their new roles in the federation as political tensions increased. Singapore, in particular, which had a sizable Chinese community, was a political hotspot. The dynamics between the People's Action Party (PAP) of Singapore and the United Malays National Organisation (UMNO) of Malaya were intricate and fraught with racial politics. The PAP, having won a convincing victory in the Singaporean elections, was seen as a champion of the Chinese community, while UMNO's political narrative was deeply rooted in protecting the rights and privileges of the Malays in Malaya.

Another twist in the intricate story of Malaysia's formation was the Brunei Revolt of 1962. In opposition to the sultan of Brunei's decision to join the proposed Federation of Malaysia, the North Borneo Federation's proponents staged an uprising. Spearheaded by the North Kalimantan National Army, supported by Indonesia, and associated with the leftist Brunei People's Party, the rebels objected to the merger, fearing it might lead to a loss of sovereignty over Brunei's lucrative oil deposits. The revolt was swiftly quelled by British forces, yet the underlying apprehension remained, ultimately leading Brunei to decide against joining the federation. It preferred to maintain its status quo of a protected state under British influence, with its rich oil reserves under its own control.

While there were considerable strains within the proposed federation, it was nothing compared to the fierce opposition from surrounding neighbors. President Sukarno of Indonesia, in particular, had been vocal in his objection to the creation of Malaysia, which later led to a resolute "Confrontation" (Konfrontasi) campaign. Sukarno was concerned that Indonesian hegemony in the area would be threatened by the rise of a politically and economically more powerful Malaysia right outside his door. He saw Malaysia as a potential puppet of Western colonial powers and, in protest, initiated a series of hostile actions, ranging from political rhetoric to actual armed incursions into Borneo.

Similarly, the Philippines had its reservations, primarily due to its longstanding claim over the territory of Sabah, one of the proposed states of Malaysia. This historical claim was based on past rule, and the Philippines sought to assert this claim, straining relations with Malaya.

In spite of these regional disruptions, Malaysia's formation proceeded. On September 16th, 1963, history was made when Malaysia was formally proclaimed, with Kuala Lumpur as its capital city. This historic occasion was the result of painstaking preparation, compromise, and negotiation. Sarawak, Sabah, Singapore, and Malaya were now part of a new nation. The Malaysian flag was raised, symbolizing unity and the dawn of a new era. The country's diverse population looked ahead with cautious optimism, embracing their collective identity as Malaysians.

Internationally, the reaction to the formation of Malaysia was mixed. The United Nations played a crucial role in conducting a referendum in

Sabah and Sarawak, which ultimately demonstrated the residents' preference to join Malaysia. This outcome was key to silencing some of the international criticism and legitimizing the formation of the new nation on the global stage. However, not all reactions were favorable. Indonesia continued its policy of Confrontation, resulting in several years of conflict that hindered progress in Malaysia. The Philippines withdrew its ambassador from Malaya, signaling a diplomatic protest against the inclusion of Sabah in Malaysia. The two countries suspended their diplomatic relations between September 1963 and May 1964 and again, due to the same issue, from 1968 to 1969.

Building Malaysia was like putting together a complicated jigsaw puzzle with pieces from several sets. The initial years faced a formidable task: knitting together the administrative systems of Malaya, Sabah, Sarawak, and Singapore into a functional federation. This was an undertaking that required balancing disparate legal systems, educational policies, and economic structures. Furthermore, it was an enormous struggle to foster a feeling of Malaysian identity in a population as different as the Borneo states and the cosmopolitan Singapore. For the sake of national unity, it was crucial to identify a shared ground for the diverse ethnic compositions, languages, and cultural legacies that each region contributed to the Malaysian mosaic.

As the new nation grappled with internal consolidation, it also had to quell the external threat posed by Indonesia's Confrontation. The military and diplomatic efforts to suppress this conflict were exhaustive, stretching the resources and resolve of the young nation. However, with the fall of President Sukarno and the ascent of Suharto to power in Indonesia, the tide began to turn. The Confrontation was brought to an end in 1966 through a peace agreement, leading to the normalization of relations between Malaysia and Indonesia. This allowed Malaysia to redirect its focus from territorial defense to nation-building.

On the domestic front, Singapore's position within the federation quickly became a topic of contention. The economic and racial strife were central to the brewing tensions. The city-state's predominantly Chinese population and market-driven economy contrasted starkly with the Malay-dominated and agriculturally based economies of other states. Lee Kuan Yew, Singapore's prime minister, was a staunch advocate for a society based on merit, where all citizens, regardless of race, would have equal opportunities. This vision was encapsulated in his call for a "Malaysian Malaysia," a concept that sought to move away from race-based policies toward a more inclusive national identity, treating all Malaysian citizens equally in terms of rights and opportunities.

The term "Malaysian Malaysia" was essentially a plea for the dismantling of ethnic preferences, particularly the special rights accorded to the Malay majority in the rest of Malaysia, known as bumiputera rights. These rights were part of affirmative action policies designed to improve the economic position of the bumiputera by giving them privileges in education, government employment, and business.

Singapore's push for a "Malaysian Malaysia" was, therefore, controversial, as it challenged the fundamental bumiputera policies of the Malaysian government. This created a rift, as the federal authorities viewed Singapore's stance as a direct challenge to policies meant to protect the socioeconomic interests of the Malay population, the indigenous and politically dominant group in Malaysia.

From here on, it was clear that the rifts were too deep, and the vision of a united Malaysia that included Singapore was unsustainable. And so, on August 9th, 1965, Singapore was expelled from the federation, becoming an independent republic. The separation was a painful decision for the leaders of both Malaysia and Singapore, but it was deemed necessary to ensure the stability and future prospects of the respective nations.

In the years that followed, Malaysia and Singapore went their separate ways, each forging their own destiny. The two nations still get along today.

Malaysia, now free from the strains of external conflict and internal discord, set out to unify its diverse populace and rich cultures under a single flag, striving toward a shared Malaysian identity. The end of hostilities with neighboring countries opened up a new era for development, allowing Malaysia to focus on nurturing unity and prosperity within its multicultural society.

Conclusion

In wrapping up our journey through Malaysia's past, it feels like we have walked together along a winding path from ancient, mystical kingdoms to the bustling, modern cities we see today. Malaysia's story is one of diversity and unity, a colorful patchwork of different cultures and traditions that have come together to create something truly special.

The Malay Archipelago was once just a whisper on the lips of traders and adventurers seeking the fabled wealth of the East. It grew in prominence, and its ports buzzed with the comings and goings of Indian, Arab, and Chinese merchants. They were later joined by European powers driven by their insatiable thirst for spices, tin, and rubber. Malaysia's geography carved its destiny as a crossroads for commerce and culture, a place where empires collided and fused, leaving behind a legacy that is evident in the faces of its people and the architecture of its cities.

This narrative, however, is not merely a chronicle of sultans and conflicts but also a story of the relentless human spirit. It is found in the courage of figures like Dato' Maharaja Lela, Mat Kilau, and Tok Janggut, whose valiant resistance against colonial rule is forever etched in the nation's memory. It is a tale of resilience, as seen through the trials endured during the Japanese occupation, and of triumph, as echoed in the jubilant cries of "Merdeka" in 1957.

The establishment of Malaysia in 1963 marked not an end but a new beginning—a dream of unity and prosperity that was challenged by the racial riots of 1969 yet also strengthened by the ambitious vision of the

New Economic Policy. Throughout the years, Malaysia has striven to balance growth with equity and to foster a sense of shared destiny among its people while nurturing the uniqueness of each community.

As we look back on Malaysia's history, we see the growth of a national identity called Bangsa Malaysia that includes and respects the diverse cultures of the Malay, Chinese, Indian, and indigenous communities. Yet, the history of a nation is not confined to the pages of a book; it is written daily in the lives of its citizens. As Malaysia continues to navigate the challenges of the 21st century—balancing development with sustainability, unity with diversity, and tradition with innovation—it does so with the wisdom gleaned from the past. This wisdom is a beacon that guides the nation as it forges its path, shaped by the collective aspirations of its people. Of course, the story of Malaysia is far from over; indeed, the most exciting pages have yet to be written.

If you enjoyed this book, a review on Amazon would be greatly appreciated because it would mean a lot to hear from you.

To leave a review:
1. Open your camera app.
2. Point your mobile device at the QR code.
3. The review page will appear in your web browser.

Thanks for your support!

Here's another book by Captivating History that you might like

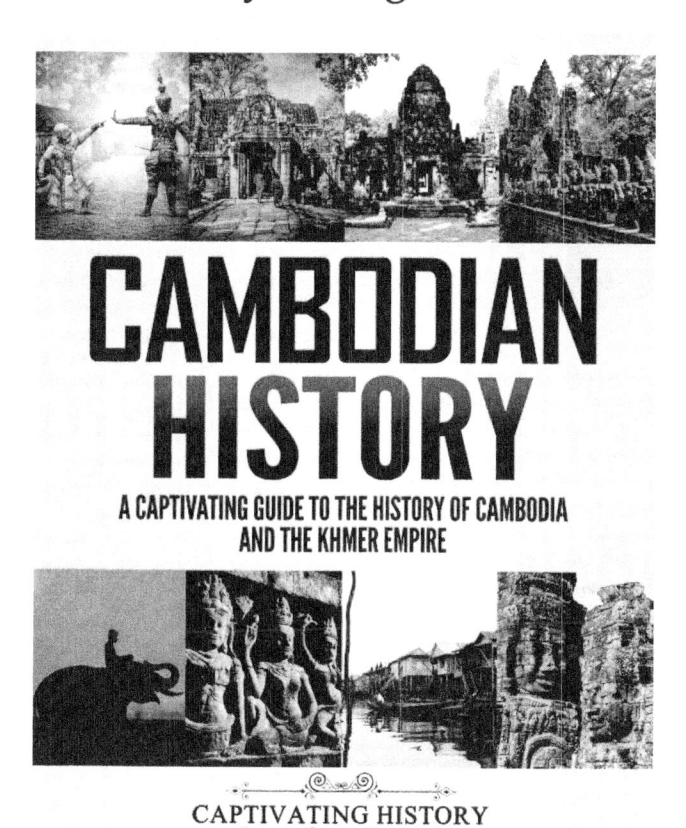

CAMBODIAN HISTORY
A CAPTIVATING GUIDE TO THE HISTORY OF CAMBODIA AND THE KHMER EMPIRE

CAPTIVATING HISTORY

Free Bonus from Captivating History (Available for a Limited time)

Hi History Lovers!

Now you have a chance to join our exclusive history list so you can get your first history ebook for free as well as discounts and a potential to get more history books for free!

Simply visit the link below to join.

Or, Scan the QR code!

captivatinghistory.com/ebook

Also, make sure to follow us on Facebook, X, and YouTube by searching for Captivating History.

Reference List

Adnan, A. S. (2015, November 30). Legasi Tuah. *Berita Harian.* https://www.bharian.com.my/amp/bhplus-old/2015/12/101137/legasi-tuah

Andaya, B. W., & Andaya, L. Y. (2016). *A History of Malaysia.* Red Globe Press.

Cartwright, M. (2023). Portuguese Malacca. *World History Encyclopedia.* https://www.worldhistory.org/Portuguese_Malacca/

C'Kay, D. (2021, August 31). *Perjuangan Mat Salleh menentang British di Borneo Utara.* The Patriots. https://www.thepatriots.asia/perjuangan-mat-salleh-menentang-british-di-borneo-utara/

Del, C. (2022, August 29). 5 Old Names Of Malaysia They Probably Didn't Teach You In School. *TRP.* https://www.therakyatpost.com/living/2022/08/29/5-old-names-of-malaysia-they-probably-didnt-teach-you-in-school/#:~:text=There%20are%20several%20records%20of,and%20Wu%2Dlai%2Dyu

Effendy, H. (2019, July 28). *Legenda Merong Mahawangsa: Hikayat berdirinya Negeri Kedah.* The Patriots. https://www.thepatriots.asia/legenda-merong-mahawangsa-hikayat-berdirinya-negeri-kedah/

History of Sarawak | Brooke Heritage Trust. (n.d.). https://www.brooketrust.org/history-of-sarawak

Invasion of Malaya. (n.d.). Australian War Memorial. https://www.awm.gov.au/collection/E84717

Japan's motives for bombing Pearl Harbor, 1941 - Association for Asian Studies. (2023, June 1). Association for Asian Studies.

https://www.asianstudies.org/publications/eaa/archives/japans-motives-for-bombing-pearl-harbor-1941/

Malayan Independence. (n.d.). History Today.
https://www.historytoday.com/archive/malayan-independence

Melaka | Dutch Trading Post Heritage Network. (n.d.). DTPHN.
https://www.dtphn.org/melaka

Patriots. (2019, October 28). *Parameswara merupakan raja India yang memeluk Islam?* The Patriots. https://www.thepatriots.asia/parameswara-merupakan-raja-india-yang-memeluk-islam/

Sandiwara. (2012, January 31). *Tun Teja: Antara Versi Sejarah Melayu dan Hikayat Hang Tuah.* SANDIWARA.
https://amnaj.wordpress.com/2012/01/30/tun-teja-antara-versi-sejarah-melayu-dan-hikayat-hang-tuah/

Sejarah Bukit Sadok dan Panglima Rentap. (2014, May 7). Utusan Borneo Online. https://www.utusanborneo.com.my/2014/05/07/sejarah-bukit-sadok-dan-panglima-rentap

The Editors of Encyclopedia Britannica. (n.d.). *Why did the atomic bombings of Hiroshima and Nagasaki happen?* Encyclopedia Britannica.
https://www.britannica.com/question/Why-did-the-atomic-bombings-of-Hiroshima-and-Nagasaki-happen

TOK JANGGUT. (2012, May 11). Tokoh Sejarah.
https://sejarahtokoh.wordpress.com/tok-janggut/

Warisan Budaya Malaysia : Sastera Rakyat. (n.d.). http://sasterarakyat-kedah.com/?cat=8

When the world came to Southeast Asia: Malacca and the Global Economy - Association for Asian Studies. (2023, June 19). Association for Asian Studies.
https://www.asianstudies.org/publications/eaa/archives/when-the-world-came-to-southeast-asia-malacca-and-the-global-economy/

Wikipedia contributors. (2023, August 1). *Ram Khamhaeng.* Wikipedia.
https://en.m.wikipedia.org/wiki/Ram_Khamhaeng

Wikipedia contributors. (2023, October 31). *Sukhothai Kingdom.* Wikipedia.
https://en.m.wikipedia.org/wiki/Sukhothai_Kingdom

Printed in Great Britain
by Amazon